# YUGOSLAVIA

## An Avoidable War

# YUGOSLAVIA

## An Avoidable War

## NORA BELOFF

Field research and photographs by BRUNO BELOFF

NEW EUROPEAN PUBLICATIONS
14-16 Carroun Road
London

Published in the United Kingdom in 1997 by
New European Publications Limited
14-16 Carroun Road
Vauxhall
London SW8 1JT
England


Cover Design: Bruno Beloff
Project Management: Simon Davie & Bruno Beloff
Typesetting: Bruno Beloff
Proof-reading: Justine Chase-Grey

British Library Cataloguing in Publication Data

ISBN 1-872410-08-1

Printed and bound in Great Britain by
Biddles Limited, Guildford and King's Lynn

# Contents

# Illustrations

## Pronounciation of Yugoslav Names

Serbo-Croat spelling of names has been used throughout, except in accepted anglicised spelling of names like Yugoslavia and Ustasha (instead of Jugoslavija and Ustaša). In Serbo-Croat, a number of consonants are designated by addition of an accents, or by the combination of two consonants. The major differences from the English pronunciation are:

| Serbo-Croat consonant | pronunciation | | | |
|---|---|---|---|---|
| c | | **ts** | in | *ts*ar |
| č | | **ch** | in | *ch*ip |
| ć | soft | **t** | in | *t*ube (similar to č, but softer) |
| dž | | **j** | in | *j*ar |
| dj | | | | (similar to dž, but softer) |
| j | | **y** | in | *y*es |
| lj | soft | **l** | in | mi*ll*ion |
| nj | soft | **n** | in | *n*ew |
| š | | **sh** | in | *sh*e |
| ž | soft | **s** | in | lei*s*ure |
| g | | **g** | in | *g*ive |

## Acknowledgements

Nora Beloff died in February 1997, having just completed the final substantive version of *Yugoslavia: An Avoidable War*. Corrections were undertaken by her nephew and researcher Bruno Beloff, with the assistance of Aleksa Gavrilović.

Nora Beloff began work on the text at the start of 1993, although her research work had begun two decades earlier: her preceding book, *Tito's Flawed Legacy,* was published in 1984. As a result, Nora Beloff had one of the most useful address books in the Balkans, with many of her established contacts having become leading players, both across the conflicts, and within the diplomatic groups which pursued them. The following four years were taken up as much by her efforts in arguing her case to those players as in compiling the following text. As a result, assembling any acknowledgements proved to be a somewhat arbitrary process. A great many people came in contact with Nora during those four years. None are likely to have forgotten the experience, and Nora listened carefully to all of them.

Dominic Flessati, who died in 1996, deserves special mention: his unique historical knowledge, eye for detail and clear-headed analysis was available throughout the process of researching the book; it might not have been completed without him.

Some of the following agree with Nora's thesis, others do not, but they all played an important role: His Excellency Robert Barnett, Paul Beaver, Martin Bell MP, Sir Nicholas Bonsor Bart. MP, Lord Carrington, His Excellency Charles Crawford, Miriam Fleishman, Marko Gašić, Aleksa Gavrilović OBE, Zaga Gavrilović, Mirijana Harding, Brigadier General de Vere Hayes, the late Major Archie Jack, Jane Lumsden, General Lewis MacKenzie, Edward Pearce, Jonathan Rooper, Lieutenant-General Sir Michael Rose, Michael Shuttleworth, and Zoran Stanković.

Blocked railway line from Osijek to southern Hungary.
UN PA Sector East. January 1993.

# Foreword

This is a remarkable book by a remarkable woman. To become the first of her gender to achieve distinction as a foreign correspondent was in itself a considerable achievement; and without courage, intellect, a thorough study of international relations as well as a determination to be objective, it would have been impossible. She had all those qualities; her critics could never deny it. More to the point, those four qualities led her to write this book. In doing so, some will doubt whether she employed the last of those four qualities.

To be objective one must at least begin with an open mind and a readiness to understand both sides of a dispute. To act otherwise is plainly to be prejudiced, in the true sense of the word. Yet from the very moment Yugoslavia began to disintegrate, we were led to believe that the Serbs were the guilty party. About the Serbian point of view there was scarcely a murmur in any part of the media. Commentators and reporters of TV, radio, newspapers and every journal with space to spare on foreign affairs all whistled the same tune. Bosnia and Croatia, good; Serbia, bad.

Just one voice tried to be heard above the clamour. Nora Beloff was saying to her friends, it is not so simple as that; it is not a case of black and white. Her friends listened, but the media denied her. They preferred the reports of a host of journalists, most of whom travelled to what was Yugoslavia for the first time in their lives, and went with little or no knowledge of her turbulent history, or understanding of the many complex and conflicting factors that had led up to her disintegration. Like a judge who hears only the plaintiff's case, they had no difficulty in finding against the defendant.

If nothing else, this book shows that the author knew an immense amount about Yugoslavia and her peoples, perhaps as much as anyone in the West. That her views were not actively sought by the Foreign Office, the State Department or the Quai d'Orsay (each of which knew her as an expert in Eastern European affairs) makes one a trifle suspicious; and suspicions multiply when all branches of the media turn a deaf ear to someone they have acknowledged as a distinguished foreign correspondent, the doyenne of her profession. Normally, when a crisis breaks out in some corner of the world, the researchers for our TV programme track down the experts, inviting them to come into the studios and pontificate to the millions. And from their desks the reporters of Fleet Street ask them for what they call "background" and a crisp quotation. Our author is no longer with us to tell us at first-hand what happened. It seems, though, that her views were not for them.

Why was this? Was it, perhaps, the purpose of the Foreign Office to defend the policy of the European Union as predetermined by Germany? I can think of one explanation. In about 1971, when Edward Heath was trying hard to get Britain into what was called the Common Market, I had lunch with the diplomatic correspondent of a well-known newspaper. We met at noon and at 3 pm cups of coffee were still being drunk. I had learnt already that he had not been to his Fleet Street office that morning, and as we were some two miles away, I asked him whether he ought not to begin his days work. "Oh, no,", he replied, "I can do it in half an hour." This rather shattered my belief that he spent his time either charging around embassies or making transnational calls to his contacts in faraway capitals. He went on to claim that a diplomatic correspondent had the easiest job on the newspaper. The Foreign Office could brief him daily; the facts they gave would be indisputable, but they were selected and only one inference could be drawn from them, namely that government policy was correct. Regurgitating the brief would take no more than half-an-hour, to embellish it perhaps an hour. "You know," he said, "that all the other papers would say the same, so no-one would contradict what you had said. This also pleased the editor, for it cut down on expenses." He added that there was no point in getting an independent story unless it was different, then it was likely to be challenged by those in high places, perhaps the Foreign Secretary himself, in a telephone call to the editor, so even if the independent story could be proved eventually to be the truth, it was easier to play safe and march in step with all the other diplomatic correspondents. "Is that why all Fleet Street is ramming down our throats that we must join the Common Market?" I asked. "Of course!" came the reply.

I had just read F A Hayek's *Road to Serfdom*, written some twenty years previously. Towards the end of the book he warns of what will happen to freedom of speech and our ability to discuss political issues if governments have more than a limited degree of power over the economy. The more a government intervenes in our lives in education, health, transport, environment etc., the more it generates news stories; and as of necessity it is the source of these stories, journalists must keep on good terms with the people providing them with the news they must write about. The more sympathetic a journalist is to his source, the more help he is likely to be given. Once interventionism passes a certain point, argued Professor Hayek, a journalist's job may depend upon his sympathetic handling of the policy.

I am not claiming that this must be the explanation why Nora Beloff was not heard. Readers can judge for themselves, having put down the book whether the possibility becomes a probability. What is a certainty is that she would never have, in a state of some desperation, sat down and written it if her message had been allowed to go forth on the media's page or screen. It is certain because her publishers were told so in the plainest terms; and what is more, she would spend her own money on promoting the book. Is she the first foreign correspondent to go so far?

The dispatches sent to *The Times* from Crimea by the first of the war correspondents, William Howard Russell, showed how public opinion could be shaped by skilful journalism. His reports, by definition, were unanimous. The reports from Bosnia have had an unanimity also, which has likewise had a deep impression upon public opinion. Nora Beloff never doubted their reports and nothing, I believe, in this book challenges the general thrust of what they have said. It has been their lot to witness a terrible tragedy; and for us in the comfort of our own homes to realise it has happened on a continent we share with the victims, is to galvanise us out of any complacency.

For our feelings to be moved is not, therefore, enough. That it has happened so close to the borders of a Union of which we have become a part should stir us to ask why this tragedy has come about, and to learn the lessons from it.

Nora Beloff has left behind a book that does both of those things. The critics will call her pro-Serb; she has not sought to be pro or anti any of the participants in the tragedy, but to do her job as foreign correspondent, steeped in the study of international relations, an expert in this part of the world, and someone determined to be objective.

The evidence laid before her readers leads her to point the accusing finger at Germany and the European Union. There is a lesson to be learnt there for all of us now deemed to be citizens of the Union. There are others to blame, too; Hitler, Stalin, Tito and other less guilty men have contributed to the tragedy. The evidence is in the following pages: it is well told and, in telling it, Nora Beloff deserves our gratitude. Let no-one pontificate about Yugoslavia's tragedy until they have read the legacy she has left behind for us.

Sir Richard Body MP
July 1997.

Women at mobile UNPROFOR checkpoint.

Near East Mostar, Bosnia and Hercegovina. 20 April 1994.

# Prologue

# The Alternative View

In the West, the generally accepted thesis is that Yugoslavia collapsed from within. The alternative view is the reverse: the Western governments, in recognising the new statelets of Croatia, Slovenia, Macedonia and Bosnia and Hercegovina, defied earlier commitments. In 1975 the European countries, the US and Canada signed the Final Act at Helsinki. This laid it down that the international frontiers of all the signatories — of which Yugoslavia was one — could not be altered without the specific agreement of the states involved and of the people living there. In practice, neither the Yugoslav federal government nor the peoples of Yugoslavia as a whole were ever properly consulted. By the 1990s, most Yugoslavs were urbanised and increasingly consumer-minded. Had they been asked for their views, the overwhelming majority would certainly have preferred peaceful negotiations to the predicted civil war.

Events in Yugoslavia, however, can only be understood within the international perspective. And it is on this point that I would claim that my lifetime experience has provided me with rare, perhaps unique, opportunities to see how, why and where major countries make the crucial decisions.

In pitting myself against the widely accepted view about the reasons why Yugoslavia collapsed in the manner in which it did, I must start by listing my own qualifications. The basic thesis which this twelve-part book will sustain is that, had it not been for the ignorance, arrogance and intrusion of the outside world, the conflicts in Yugoslavia could have been averted and, in some form, the state of Yugoslavia preserved. I claim this despite the fact — discussed later in the book — that the Yugoslav federation was becoming increasingly shaky.

This book does not set out to defend any single one of the warring groups and I approach the issue not as a "Yugoslavia expert" but as a highly experienced specialist on international affairs. Indeed, I did not visit Yugoslavia at all until 1979, by which time I had already investigated all the other communist countries and had written a book predicting the collapse and dissolution of the USSR [1].

It is unnecessary here to go into the details about when and where I travelled. But I must pinpoint the essential missions, which justify my claim to exceptional experience of the way in which various governments and institutions function. First, from before the end of World War Two until the present time, I have frequently visited France and regard Paris as my second home. Having had a French governess since the age of four, I grew up bilingual and, after graduating with a history degree from Oxford, I was assigned to the French section of the Foreign Office's political Intelligence Department. Immediately after the liberation of Paris, I was given the temporary status of diplomat and flown out to France where I worked under the ambassador, Duff Cooper. It was from Paris that I watched the creation and consolidation of the Fourth Republic.

After conscription ended, I chose to go into journalism, starting in the Paris offices of Reuters and then *The Economist*. Since that time, I have never lost interest in the French political scene and, in recent years, more particularly on how French policy has evolved towards Yugoslavia. Nevertheless, like anyone else concerned with world events, my principal preoccupation has had to be with Washington DC. It is there, and only there, that the vital intergovernmental decisions are taken — or dodged.

In 1949 *The Observer* named me their Washington correspondent and, for the rest of my journalistic career, I acted as a yo-yo, going to the United States as often as required. I was an accredited member of the White House press corps for varying lengths of time, under all presidents from Truman to Carter. Since then, I have frequently gone to the United States and Canada, though no longer representing a newspaper.

Equally important to me has been my experience of working in Moscow. This goes back to 1956, when I first went to the USSR accompanying the then French Prime Minister, Guy Mollet. I served as Moscow correspondent during Nikita Khrushchev's time, although only intermittently: I was never granted a residential permit. Later, I made many more visits to territories controlled from Moscow. The last two visits were in 1991: the first before, the second after, the collapse of the USSR.

Another vital ingredient in my experience has been the reporting of the creation and buildup of the European Community (EC). As a personal friend of Jean Monnet, I had seen the origins of the new Europe and, in 1963, the EC was the subject of my first book [2]. It described how and why General De Gaulle vetoed the British application for entry into the then six-state community. And so, in the summer of 1991, when the now enlarged Community first intruded into Yugoslav affairs, I was well placed to assess how each power put its domestic interests first. I protested at the time against the arrogance and ignorance of non-Yugoslav intruders who were fatal to the preservation of peace.

Those who made foreign policy at the time can plead extenuating circumstances. In 1989, after the destruction of the Berlin Wall and the dissolution of the power structures all over Eastern Europe, the fall of Yugoslavia seemed only part of the picture. The death of Yugoslavia was proclaimed first by the EC, led by Germany, and later by the USA, which, at the time, controlled a majority in the United Nations (UN).

It is true that by 1991 the Yugoslav federal government was struggling for its existence. What made the struggle hopeless was the decision of the EC to prevent the Yugoslav federation from having recourse to its own armed forces in order to preserve the state of Yugoslavia. Under the contemporary and politically correct belief in the wickedness of the use of armed force, this seemed synonymous with favouring peace. In reality, as this policy was applied in Yugoslavia, it turned out to be the reverse.

The case in favour of preserving Yugoslavia, the union of South Slavs, was inherent in its creation in 1918. The territories involved were all reacting against having been colonised either by the Ottoman or Hapsburg Empires. They had thus managed to form a single country which the leaders hoped would be able to defend its international interests. Though living within a single state, the peoples of Yugoslavia nonetheless clung to their religious, cultural and traditional differences. In some parts of a country roughly the size of France, the residents belonged to the same national / tribal group. But there were many highly populous regions, north, south, east and west, where the communities lived on top of each other. Catholic, Orthodox, and Muslim peoples lived not only in the same towns and villages but often in the same blocks of flats and there were millions of mixed marriages.

With this degree of intermingling, the governance of Yugoslavia was never going to be easy. And, indeed, the history of royalist Yugoslavia (1918-1941) was both turbulent and stressful. Yet, as the record shows, it would be wrong to assume that it was the inner contradictions of royalist Yugoslavia which in 1941 led to its collapse. In reality, it was the German blitzkrieg which smashed Yugoslavia as easily as it had smashed Poland.

The alternative to peaceful coexistence within a single Yugoslav state, both in 1918, when Yugoslavia was formed, and in 1991, when its component parts seceded, could only be civil war. The difference in 1991 was that some of the big powers, for reasons arising from domestic policies of their own, were this time encouraging the breakdown of Yugoslavia. In practice, the EC prevented the peoples of Yugoslavia from defending themselves.

If Yugoslavia had held together, the Serb communities, of which one quarter under Tito's dispensation lived outside Serbia proper, would have continued to operate within a single country. In the generally accepted view, the refusal of the Serbs from outside Serbia to become foreigners in what they regarded as their own country was dismissed as evidence of expansionist aspirations towards a "Greater Serbia". The alternative view defended in this book is that these communities had every right to reject submission, either to Franjo Tuđman's Croatia or to Alija Izetbegović's Bosnia and Hercegovina. In all the newly recognised statelets, the Serbs would have constituted a vulnerable minority. Most Serbs outside Serbia justified resistance to this plight, even if this required the use of armed force

Given the climate of opinion, anyone accepting the alternative view risks being denounced as "pro-Serb". This has happened not only to me but to David Binder of *The New York Times*, to the German writer Peter Handke and to many others. Such *ad hominem* attacks may well indicate an awareness of the flimsy basis of most of the comment. This book not only refutes allegations that I am more "pro-Serb" than "pro" any other group. It also points out the reasons why, had it not been for misguided foreign intrusion, the Yugoslav catastrophe need never have taken place.

**Footnotes**

1. Beloff, Nora (1979). *Inside the Soviet Empire: Myth and Reality.* New York Times Books.

2. Beloff, Nora (1963). *The General Says No.* Penguin. The following year the book was translated into *French: Le General Dit Non.* Les Editions Plon, Paris.

Bosnian Serb farmer.
Trnovo, Republika Srpska. 13 May 1994.

# 1

# Tito's Poisoned Legacy

By the time Josip Broz, alias Tito, died in 1980, the state of Yugoslavia was already in an advanced state of disintegration. For 36 years Tito had been both head of the Yugoslav Communist Party and head of state, and his leadership was undisputed. It was during this time that the ground had been laid for the subsequent conflicts. Yet in the West the damage Tito had inflicted went virtually unnoticed. In 1948 Stalin had excommunicated Tito's Yugoslavia from the family of communist countries and, from then on, in Western eyes he could do no wrong. In reality, once Khrushchev succeeded Stalin, Belgrade and Moscow were reconciled and for the rest of his life Tito retained closer contacts with the USSR than with the West. Yet, in Western capitals, "Titoism", which included financial and diplomatic support for Tito himself, went unchallenged. Long after the cult of the leader had waned in Yugoslavia itself, Western chanceries, notably the British FCO, clung to the Titoist mythology.

Tito had taken over a country ravaged by war. No European state had suffered similar losses: the deaths are estimated to have numbered about a million. The exceptional degree of violence in the present conflict can only be understood by going back to 1941, and Hitler's genocidal decision to rank the Serbs with the Jews and Gypsies as a people to be destroyed. As part of his wartime strategy Hitler had initially decided that he would force

Yugoslavia to join the Axis, and at the beginning of 1941 it looked as if he had succeeded. Paul, the Prince Regent, went to meet Hitler in Berlin and agreed conditionally (but would Hitler have respected the conditions?) to take Yugoslavia into the Axis.

To Hitler's rage, however, when Prince Paul returned home the Serb garrison in Belgrade organised a putsch, deposed the Prince Regent and recognised the young King Peter, though still not of age, to be the reigning monarch. It was on this occasion that an enchanted Churchill declared that "Yugoslavia had found its soul."

Having execrated the Serbs, Hitler left the job of implementing his genocidal intentions to his foreign minister, Joachim Ribbentrop. After some disputes between various Nazi factions, Ribbentrop decided to appoint Ante Pavelić to take over Croatia on Germany's behalf. Pavelić had been inculpated in the murder of King Alexander of Yugoslavia in 1934 and belonged to the extremist right-wing organisation named the Ustasha. Representing only a marginal group, he had been forced to flee and had found asylum with Mussolini. Ribbentrop brought him back from Italy and put him in charge of a Greater Croatia, which included the provinces of Bosnia and Hercegovina and a part of Vojvodina. He remained in power until Germany's defeat.

When the Germans carved up Yugoslavia, the neighbouring countries shared the spoils and helped to repress the Serbs. After the blitzkrieg and the occupation of Yugoslavia, the resistance movements rallied around two leaders: Draža Mihailović, who had been an officer in the royalist army and represented continuity, and the communist leader, Tito, who organised and commanded the Partisans.

During the Molotov / Ribbentrop pact (1939-1941), Tito, like all the good communists, supported the Axis. He wrote articles repeatedly denouncing the Allies as warmongers and accused them of dragging Yugoslavia into war. After the German invasion of the USSR in June 1941, everything changed. From then on Tito, like Stalin himself and under Stalin's orders, needed both Western support and Western recognition. The Partisans quickly aligned themselves with the Allies and learnt to use language acceptable in the West. As the war drew on and the Red Army was doing most of the fighting, such somersaults were quickly forgotten and forgiven. The pro-communist climate in the West opened the way to the infiltration of Western intelligence. By early 1943 Western powers started to concentrate their support on the Partisans, and Tito induced them to dump Mihailović, which they did officially in February 1944.

While Tito was still pro-Axis, it was Mihailović who had initiated resistance. As an officer in the Yugoslav army he had foreseen the occupation and, as British officers knew, had favoured preparing for guerilla war. He saw himself as the representative of the exiled government and hoped that any Yugoslav willing to resist would rally to him. It was only after his personal contact with Tito, in July 1941, that he realised that the communists' war aims differed fundamentally from his own and that the Partisans intended to oppose him by military and civilian means.

At first, Tito's Partisans operated in Serbia proper, but within a few months they were driven out and he was forced to evacuate his diminutive units into Western Bosnia and Croatia. The Partisans in these regions recruited the Serb survivors of the Ustasha massacres and they became the largest component of the Partisan army. Hardly any of the Serbs fighting inside the Partisan ranks knew or cared about Tito's revolutionary intentions. What they were seeking was the leadership provided by Tito's mobile units. For this reason there were Serbs fighting both with Mihailović and with Tito.

While resistance inside Yugoslavia was split, furious quarrels broke out within the exiled government in London. The Croat ministers flatly refused to accept accounts of crimes perpetrated by fellow-Croats and the continuous arguments between Serb and Croat ministers paralysed the London government. Aware of the collision, the Western powers agreed that the centralist system of government, which had prevailed under the monarchy, could not be revived. Instead, it was hoped that postwar Yugoslavia would adopt a decentralised, federal form of government, granting autonomy to the various communities.

The Allied pressure for a federal government was accepted by both the resistance groups. As Tito acquired the archives, little is known about the Mihailović side. But a former British Liaison Officer (BLO), Major Archie Jack, revealed to me that he was personally entrusted with the task of delivering a federal proposal from Mihailović's supporters to the West. A congress of Mihailović's followers convened at the village of Ba in January 1944 and adopted a federal resolution. Many of those assembled had risked their lives making the journey. By this time however, the communists, well entrenched in the British services, had no difficulty in ridiculing and denying the authenticity of the Ba Congress. Jack took the federal resolution as far as Bari in Italy, but after the war he discovered that it had never reached London.

For Tito, as for Stalin, the word "federation" presented no difficulties. It was useful propaganda, though in the Western meaning of the term, federation was always incompatible with the realities of communist rule. What Westerners assume to be a necessary prerequisite of federation is an independent judiciary and compulsory limitations on the powers of central government. No communist leader would tolerate such infringements of party power.

Given Tito's dependence on the Allied support, he made no difficulty in declaring that his Yugoslavia would be "federal". Any federation needs border lines to separate its constituent components and Tito left map-making to his aides. Personally, he tended to be dismissive about the importance of these "administrative" lines. According to Milovan Djilas, Tito said: "With us [meaning the Communist Party], these demarcation lines will be no more than administrative frontiers" [1]. At that time Tito still accepted a basic tenet of Marxist-Leninist dogma: in the communist Utopia, men would identify themselves not with nationalities but with class. But Tito was a quick learner and it did not take long, once he was in the seat of government, for him to see that the Marxist dogma had no relation to reality.

The three men to whom Tito left the job of map-making were Milovan Djilas, Edvard Kardelj and Alexander Ranković. Djilas, from Montenegro, was close to Tito. Kardelj, a former schoolmaster, was a Slovene. It was only much later that it was revealed how Slovene he had felt while the maps were being drawn. Ranković was a Serb by origin but as rootless as most of the other leading communists. Ranković was head of Tito's secret police and when the BLO Bill Hudson first visited Tito's headquarters in Užice (Serbia), in autumn 1941, Ranković had already installed his service in the basement. Hudson recalled hearing the screams of people being tortured or executed.

The outward appearance of legitimacy was provided by a council, in lieu of a parliament, which came to be known as AVNOJ. Like all assemblies convened by the Communist Party, its only task was to endorse the leader's edicts.

The best study of the map-makers' guidelines was completed in many years of study by the Serb scholar, Kosta Čavoški. His conclusions were published for the first time in the West by the Paris journal *Dialogue* [2]. The border lines, as he showed, were drawn from historical precedents, but in order to get the politically desirable results, the dates to which such history referred were remarkably varied. As the historian Ivan Avakumović has recalled, the borders of Bosnia and the eastern borders of Croatia were redrawn on five separate occasions in the first part of the twentieth century [3]. Those of Dalmatia, now part of Croatia, were reconfigured six times during the same period. In some cases these borders went back to before the Congress of Berlin in 1878, whereas others had been drawn more recently. In some contested areas the decisions were left in abeyance and territorial disputes have lasted until today.

For the map-makers, Croatia was the most awkward issue. On the one side they had to satisfy the Croat communists, who had their own separatist agenda; on the other, the rest of Tito's Yugoslavia could not be ignored. The Croats themselves had been traditionally divided between those who favoured Yugoslavia and those who favoured an all-Croat state. The plans for a Union of South Slavs, which became Yugoslavia, were initiated by liberal Croats in the mid-Nineteenth century. The other strand of Croat opinion favoured a racially "pure" Croatia from which non-Croats would be excluded.

During the occupation, the Nazis had given Pavelić the whole of Bosnia and Hercegovina. The map-makers decided that this was excessive and declared the two provinces to be a separate "republic". The national / cultural identity of those who lived there was undefined. It was not until the 1960s that Tito decided that the Bosnian Muslims had the right to a separate national — not only religious — identity. From the 1950s, Tito had been promoting a new international grouping known as the "non-aligned" movement. The movement still exists, though it has lost most of its prestige. The other initiators were Pandit Nehru and the Egyptian dictator, General Abdul Nasser. The group, which soon acquired an anti-Western or, as they saw it, anti-colonial stance, grew to command a substantial portion of the UN General Assembly.

By the 1960s much of Tito's foreign policy was designed to improve relations with the Islamic world and he now agreed to recognise the Bosnian Muslims as a community in its own right. This meant, for the first time, giving a religious connotation to identify a national grouping. From the 1960s the term "Muslim" (with a capital M) enabled Bosnian Muslims to claim to be one of Bosnia's constituent communities. Tito knew that Bosnia could not be governed as a unitary state. His solution was to impose a power-sharing formula: all the major institutions, including newspapers and universities, would be managed by a collective body representing all three communities.

Though the map-makers deprived Croatia of Bosnia and Hercegovina, they decided that the Croat boundaries would include the border region of Krajina, populated mainly by Serbs. These had arrived in this province in the course of sixteenth and seventeenth centuries, invited by the Hapsburgs, and were given land and privileges in return for military service against the Turks. During the Second World War, Krajina had witnessed some of the worst Ustasha atrocities and, as we know now, the decision to incorporate it into Croatia did not go unchallenged. One of Tito's closest friends, Moše Pijade, had been in Krajina during the war.

He warned that, after what had happened, the province would never willingly accept to be administered from Zagreb.

In the 1930s Pijade and Tito had served in prison together and, according to Tito, Pijade had taught the prospective party leader the ABC of Marxist-Leninism during their joint imprisonment. Before his imprisonment, Tito had been an uneducated agitator pushing for Croat independence. He might never have qualified as Stalin's choice for the Yugoslav party's Secretary General if Pijade had not helped him to master communist dogma. On Krajina, however, Pijade was overruled by Djilas, who insisted that, without Krajina, Croatia would be unacceptably divided.

The borders of Slovenia presented no similar difficulties. Under Kardelj's guidance, borders of the prewar Slovenia were extended to include the port of Kope and the hinterland of Trieste. (In 1945 the Partisans had failed to grab Trieste from the Allies). Postwar Slovenia also took over the northern province of Gorizia, acquired from the defeated Italians.

For a time, Tito hesitated about whether to make the intra-federal lines permanent or provisional. The centrifugal forces at first seemed to prevail and the communists let it be known that any republic would be free to secede. Later, Tito decided that the secession of any part of his Yugoslavia would gravely weaken his own status. It was left to Moše Pijade to explain the reversal of the communist line. This he did in Belgrade in 1946, at what was called "the constituent assembly", which had replaced AVNOJ. He claimed that the borders had been drawn "with the blood of the resistance heroes" and that any tampering with their work would amount to betraying their legacy.

Tito, of course, did not rely on persuasion. From the moment he took power he introduced a reign of terror, behind an impenetrable iron curtain, which virtually smashed opposition. A Polish communist recalled having been scolded for the failure of the Poles to smash opposition, and Stalin quoted Tito as an example which other communists should follow. Hundreds of thousands of Yugoslavs were killed and some million went in and out of Tito's prisons. Tito had regarded himself as the best Stalinist in the business and, as he said later, when Stalin denounced him in 1948, he felt he had been struck by a thunderbolt. It was true that Tito had followed an activist foreign policy but, as he saw it, always with the purpose of extending Stalin's power [4].

After failing to grab Trieste, Tito sent Yugoslav Macedonians into Greece to support the communist rebellion. Meanwhile, the West was beginning to react, and President Truman underwrote the non-communists in Turkey and Greece. Stalin could not allow Tito to risk a world war and decided to replace him with a more amenable leader. As we now know from Khrushchev, Stalin had wrongly supposed that getting rid of Tito would require no more than the shaking of a finger.

At first, Tito imitated Stalin's centralist policy. But, confronted with peasant opposition, this had to be revised or the peasants would have refused to feed the towns. And, gradually, a new system of delegating power to local communists prevailed. Power and patronage were lavished on those notably named by Djilas the "Red Barons". The criteria for the selection of the Barons was their degree of fealty; when this seemed in question, they could always be purged and replaced. The Barons were allowed to bestow rewards on their own clientele and build up their own separate economies. The consequence was to place each of the "republics" in competition with its neighbours, which soon became its rivals.

In the years before his death (1980), Tito publicly lamented the development of eight separate "autarchies" (the six "Republics" and two "Autonomous Regions") and declared that their rivalry with each other was ruining the state of Yugoslavia. Nevertheless, he refrained from demanding that any of the Barons should submit to any federal authority but his own.

"Is Yugoslavia a single country?" was the question put to me in 1985, while Tito's successors were still in office. A few bankers in the City of London were putting together a syndicated loan for a Yugoslav enterprise and, knowing that I was specialising on this part of the world, had consulted me. My answer had to be: "No, it is not." Yet, although businessmen recognised from their own experiences that Yugoslavia was falling apart, the same message failed to reach Western chanceries, notably the FCO and the State Department. These went on seeing Tito and his communist successors as the best guarantors of Yugoslav unity.

In terms of propaganda, the Yugoslav communists have been formidably successful. Once he controlled the archives, Tito had built up an entirely fictitious version of Yugoslavia's wartime history, which he managed to sell to most Western observers. Tito's founding myth was that Tito, under his "brotherhood and unity" slogan, had overcome Yugoslavia's nationality problems. In reality, Tito had threatened to prosecute anyone daring to express nationalist feelings and had swept such feelings under the carpet.

Though Titoist terror subsided, the memories remained. Many potential opponents of the totalitarian rule managed to emigrate. Those who could not leave were careful to say nothing critical of the leader. One outlet for malcontents rested in the differences of opinion between the Red Barons. Thus the novelist Dobrica Ćosić was prohibited from publishing his works in Belgrade but given enthusiastic acclaim when his novels came out in the Croat city of Rijeka.

In the years immediately following the last war, Tito, like other communist leaders, did not have to worry about economic growth. Peasants were pouring into the cities and providing an ample and docile labour force. By the mid-1960s, however, the boom had collapsed and Tito, in desperate need of hard currency, decided to allow Yugoslav workers to go to the West and earn deutchmarks or other convertible currencies. This set him apart from the rest of the communist world, which feared the consequences of any opening to the West. Tito, though anxious to impress westerners with his liberal image, took all the necessary precautions inside Yugoslavia to prohibit the faintest criticisms of his regime. Even private conversations could lead to the prosecution of the speakers. Known intellectuals had their homes bugged by the secret police and political conversations could only take place in the open air.

Tito's Yugoslavia had four constitutions, all drafted by Edvard Kardelj. The last, promulgated in 1974, was not only the longest (408 articles) but also the most centrifugal. Tito had himself elected for life but he made sure that nobody after him would step into his shoes and, as an international statesman, straddle the world.

The last constitution laid it down that, after Tito's death, leadership would rotate: the communities would take their turn in providing a "President of the Presidency". The text also provided that each of the separate "republics" would exercise a veto on any major federal decisions. In other words, central government was paralysed.

Yet, for a whole decade after Tito's death, Yugoslavia stayed united under communist control: inertia and vested interests prevailed. It was not until 1990, when communism was collapsing all over Eastern Europe, that the Yugoslav Communist Party fell apart. Yet, right through the 1980s, Western governments and most of Western opinion favoured communist rule, believing it to be the cement holding Yugoslavia together. Western governments welcomed the survival of Titoism as something of a miracle. "The West would have paid billions of dollars to preserve Titoism and now it looks as if we are getting it for free." These words were spoken in 1985 by a former British ambassador to Yugoslavia, in the corridors of the Royal Institute of International Affairs. He was walking with another diplomat to a meeting on Yugoslavia. Having heard the remark, I knew that the West was in for a catastrophic surprise.

**Footnotes**

1. Djilas, Milovan (22 March 1984). *Osmica.*

2. Čavoški, Kosta (April 1995). *Dialogue.*

3. Avakumović, Ivan (1996). The Bully on the Block: American Policy in the Former Yugoslavia. *Second Annual Regional Conference on Russian, East European and Central Asian Studies*, University of Washington, Seattle.

4. Tito's reactions are described in: Djilas, Milovan (1980). *Tito: The Story from Inside.* Harcourt Brace Jovanovich.

Boy playing near World War Two memorial.
Kragujevac, Serbia. April 1993.

# 2

# How Tito's Federal Borders became International Frontiers

Almost fifty years after Tito's map-makers had cobbled together the borders of Tito's "federation", Western governments decided to metamorphose these into frontiers of internationally-recognised states. On 22 May 1992 a plenary session of the UN General Assembly welcomed by acclaim the new states of Slovenia, Croatia and Bosnia with Hercegovina within their Titoist administrative boundaries.

As the present conflict in Yugoslavia drew on, Western governments were ready to endorse these highly disputable lines not only by diplomatic means but also to commit UN and, later, NATO troops to impose them by force. Outside intervention in Yugoslav affairs, which began in earnest in the summer of 1991, aggravated and exacerbated the conflict. The Unilateral Declarations of Independence (UDI) by Slovenia and Croatia were interpreted to mean that the state of Yugoslavia was already finished. Yet all the countries involved had signed the Final Act at Helsinki in 1975, in which existing frontiers, including the frontiers of the state of Yugoslavia (itself a signatory), could not be changed without the consent of the governments and peoples concerned. In Yugoslavia's case, neither the federal government of Yugoslavia nor the peoples living in Yugoslavia were ever comprehensively consulted.

After the fall of the Berlin Wall, Western leaders betrayed an astounding degree of euphoria about notions of a "New Europe". In November 1990 the former British Prime Minister, Margaret Thatcher, declared that she favoured "a Magna Carta" designed to entrench basic freedoms for every individual. Thanks to her enthusiasm, a conference was called in Paris (March 1992) and a "Paris Charter" echoed her ecstasy:

"The era of confrontation and division of Europe has ended... Ours is a time for fulfilling the hopes and expectations our peoples have cherished for decades: steadfast commitment to democracy based on human rights and fundamental freedoms; prosperity through economic liberty and social justice; and equal security for all our countries."

It was true that, as the cold war appeared to have ended, the world did confront a new and different Europe. The institutions which had developed during the East / West deadlock now needed new missions. It was unfortunate for the peoples of Yugoslavia that the EU chose to exploit the impending Yugoslav crisis as an occasion to show that it was capable of preserving peace anywhere in Europe. In practice, it showed the reverse.

The most detailed, day-to-day account of the EU's involvement has been provided by the chief Dutch negotiator, Henry Wynaendts [1]. His book concedes that most Europeans dreaded being sucked into the Balkan quagmire, but the indispensability of an EU presence was something Wynaendts and his immediate collaborators declared themselves "sure" of. In order to assert itself, the still embryonic EU was, in their view, morally obliged to commit itself.

The EU's involvement followed a recognised EU institutional format. A "Troika" was sent in, in this case from Holland, Portugal and Luxembourg: Hans Van den Broek, Jao Pinhero and Jacques Poos. None of the three had the faintest idea of what was really going on in the Yugoslavia into which they recklessly allowed themselves to be sucked. Their ignorance and incapacity was later confirmed by Willy Claes, at that time the Belgian Foreign Minister. In a conversation with me, he suggested that, in future, any EU Troika should always include at least one representative of a big power; only these had Yugoslav experts within their ministries.

The Dutch, including Wynaendts, fell in with the German view that Yugoslavia should be abolished and that the new states of Croatia and Slovenia should be internationally recognised. Every time members of the mission went to Belgrade and met any Serbs, they were repeatedly warned that the Serbs would resist any settlement which left Serb communities under the control of Franjo Tuđman's Croatia, and later of Izetbegović's Bosnia. They heard but refused to listen. Instead, before Wynaendts arrived, Milošević (the president of the Serb Republic) was singled out as the villain. Those who met him attributed the war to what they claimed were his "hegemonistic" aims for a "Greater Serbia".

In Wynaendts' and the German view, Milošević could thus be identified as the true aggressor. In reality, as any study of events in Belgrade will confirm, the Serb leader never used the words "Greater Serbia", except to refute accusations made by outside powers.

An awareness that Yugoslavia was in danger of collapse had been evident to some Yugoslavs since the 1974 constitution, which left the Serb communities within sovereign Croatian and Bosnian "republics". Many pessimists from all communities began storing weapons for prospective use. By 1990 the imminent danger of civil war was widely appreciated and the exodus of refugees, mainly Serb but also Croat and Muslim, began. All were fleeing from areas where another community had a majority.

For the 1990-91 period, we get an insider's view from Borislav Jović, a close associate of Milošević and President of the Presidency during most of this time [2]. On 13 February 1990 Jović notes that "Slobodan Milošević is afraid of war", and says that he (Jović) told the American ambassador, Warren Zimmermann, that the best way of preserving Yugoslav unity was to back communist rule.

This communist view separated the ruling Serbs from the Yugoslav federal government, then led by the Croat Ante Marković. He had been an economist and took over the government in 1988. During his tenure of office he struggled to introduce private enterprise and managed the priority task of halting hyperinflation and making the dinar convertible. Marković's aim, however, was primarily political, though for a long time he went on hoping that political change could be achieved through economic reform. What he and his supporters (many of them Serb, but also Croat, Slovene and Muslim) hoped to create was a democratic Yugoslavia III — a title intended to distinguish it from royalist Yugoslavia I and Communist Yugoslavia II. In such a Yugoslavia, neither Milošević nor Jović would qualify for jobs.

By 25 March 1990, Jović was reporting that even veteran believers in a single Yugoslavia were losing their confidence. The eminent Serb writer and, later, political leader Dobrica Ćosić was now saying that there was no longer any serious reason for Yugoslavia to exist.  In the long period of communist rule,

Yugoslavia lost its economic unity and there was no common purpose among the separate "republics". Later, Ćosić was to change his mind. By October 1990, when I visited him in Belgrade, Ćosić saw that any rupture of the state of Yugoslavia was bound to lead to civil war. He told me then that "only a miracle" could prevent the descent of Yugoslavia into violence and viciousness which would be comparable to the horrors experienced during the last war.

What is most revealing in the Jović account is the revelation of how close the Yugoslav Peoples' Army (JNA) came, under its multi-ethnic leadership, to intervening militarily to preserve Yugoslav unity. Its chief, Veljko Kadijević, himself half-Croat half-Serb, favoured military action to mobilize supporters of Yugoslavia. He wanted to arrest and disarm any Yugoslav officers or men who favoured secession. In February 1991, Kadijević told Jović that the JNA must take preventative action against what he saw as a German plot to break up the Yugoslav state, which he was sure would lead to civil war. Kadijević gave Jović a written draft which would have authorised the army to treat advocates of secession as traitors. During that month, the Yugoslav intelligence services infiltrated the Croat secessionists and were able to show pictures of the Croat minister of defence, Spegelj, discussing plans to send Croat units to surround and, where necessary, to slaughter JNA officers and their families. The film was shown on Belgrade TV and created a furore.

On 6 March the Serb leaders reluctantly approved the Kadijević plan and agreed that the JNA should be free to arrest secessionists. Kadijević then flew to Moscow, but he failed to get any promise that the JNA could rely on Soviet support if it mobilized pro-Yugoslav forces. Thus, in the chaos bequeathed by Tito, Marković's federal government and, quite separately, the JNA, were both striving to prevent the collapse of Yugoslavia. Neither of them drew on international support nor on the clout of the other. All this, of course, was way beyond the comprehension of the intervening Troika.

After his visit to Moscow, Kadijević told Jović that he now felt that he no longer needed the approval of the presidency. Under Tito's regime, Tito himself controlled the JNA. Kadijević announced that, with or without political backing, he intended to arrest and disarm the secessionist leaders. According to Jović, he said: "We shall go for army strikes. Either the Presidency gives us authority for mobilising pro-Yugoslavia forces or else we will mobilize whether it agrees or not". Jović asked what Kadijević meant by "strikes". Kadijević replied: "We shall replace the government and the Presidency [Kadijević saw the army as the protector of the Yugoslav state, not of the communist leadership] and we shall indefinitely suspend the activities of Assembly, and during the next six months we shall take over responsibility for Yugoslav unity" [3]. Jović was so alarmed that he came close to resigning.

In April 1991, three months before the EU involvement, Kadijević, who had still refrained from action, rhetorically asked Jović and Milošević whether they would be willing to abandon Knin and other Serb inhabited towns. When the Serb leaders said "No," and emphatically favoured protecting the Serb communities, Jović felt that they had "crossed the Rubicon." [4]

Divisions and confusion in Belgrade were made worse by the EU's reckless intervention. Its first demand was that the JNA be prohibited from taking any action to defend Yugoslavia. No multi-ethnic country, not even France, would have been able to avert terror and violence if its army had been paralysed. Yet this was what the Troika was demanding. They reached the peak of imbecility when, in defence of Tito's 1974 constitution, they demanded that Belgrade appoint the Croat separatist Stipe Mesić to be the President of the Presidency. Mesić never concealed his intention of doing his utmost to dismember Yugoslavia and later wrote a book on his presidency entitled *How Yugoslavia was Destroyed* [5]. The demand that such a man should be imposed by an external body to be leader in Belgrade typified the futile unawareness of the EU Troika.

Given the German commitment to breaking up Yugoslavia, Marković's final attempts to avert civil war fell on deaf ears. Since Marković had taken office, Western powers had been losing confidence in Yugoslavia and, though they backed the Federal Prime Minister in principle, none of the major governments offered material support. Meanwhile, as Jović's book confirms, the Serb leaders were turning against Marković and seeing in him a threat to their own survival. Jović reveals that in March 1991 he and Milošević were plotting to destroy the Marković government. According to Jović, this would be done by "throwing out" Slovenia and Croatia from Yugoslavia, though at that time Milošević still supposed he could preserve his control over the Serb communities in Krajina.

By this time Milošević was warning that, in view of the way things were developing, the Serbs must be ready to shed blood. This was, of course, in total conflict with Marković's objective of settling the disputes by peaceful negotiation. Right until the fatal declarations of independence of Slovenia and Croatia, he went on warning against impending civil war. Marković's last plea to avert the catastrophe was delivered to highly unsympathetic delegates at the Zagreb Assembly and broadcast live [6]. The Prime Minister had travelled from Belgrade, the seat of the Federal

Government, to speak to euphoric nationalist delegates, and he pulled no punches:

"What I would like to say to you is something I have never spoken of before: where I differ from many of my critics is that love of my nation does not mean I hate or am intolerant of other peoples. Really it requires love of other nations and Yugoslavia and the world, and I only see my relationship in this way...

"If there is no willingness to discuss our problems round the table, then there is no way out ... I am sure that we are all thoroughly convinced that these are decisive and crucial moments for our country. The fate of perhaps several generations will depend on the steps by each of us and by each one who has influence on the policy of the country. No one has the right to abuse his power and provoke consequences which for a very long time to come will affect millions of our people."

Referring to his travel around Yugoslavia as Prime Minister, Marković said:

"On the basis of visits which we made, we know that arms are very much present. It is not just that the police force and some paramilitary [formations] are being armed, but completely illegal organisations, citizens are being armed. An enormous amount of arms are in the hands of both sides. Whatever arms are being accumulated, then believe me, pressure is being built for the arms to be used.

"We have not championed transformations, reforms and democratisation of our society just for our contradictions to be resolved by arms, but by democratic methods, agreements, by seeking solutions for a possible coexistence. The whole of history shows that, even after wars, parties had to sit at a negotiating table and agreements had to be concluded. In the meantime many lives were lost, lots of blood flowed. Do we need this?"

On his two central issues, Marković was prophetic. In a country where virtually every family had arms, the civil war was indeed to prove long and bloody. Further, as he expected, the collisions dragged in the outside world.

Deaf to these prophesies, Wynaendts and his colleagues were upset and shocked when, on so many occasions, Serbs and Croats broke elaborately negotiated truces. Had the Troika had a better grasp of the reasons for the conflict, and of the incompatibility of the war aims of Tuđman and the Serb leadership, it should have been easy enough to predict that each side would blame the other for the resumption of fighting.

Having decided that the Serbs had instigated the conflict, Wynaendts looked the other way rather than report Serb casualties. Thus he felt able to reveal that, by the time the EU mission arrived, the town of Gospić was largely destroyed. Yet he failed to mention that the destruction had been provoked by the arrival of a Croat / Ustasha unit and that, between 16 and 18 October, 1991, 24 resident Serbs, selected mainly from the educated elements, were found dead (around 80 others were never found). Their bodies were later identified by forensic scientists [7]. Further, though Wynaendts sticks to his German-inspired anti-Serb view, he has to reveal that in his final negotiations, it was Tuđman, and not the JNA leaders, who torpedoed negotiations.

By July 1991, Tuđman had already begun his policy of blockading and trying to starve out the JNA garrisons which were located on what he saw as Croat territories. The JNA, primarily consisting of conscripts, was composed of recruits from all the communities, and those garrisons who were primarily Croat willingly gave themselves up. Many of the rest endured the hardship and waited for the JNA to come and rescue them. Wynaendts was yearning for a peace deal and, in Belgrade, Kadijević offered him one which sounded reasonable. The proposal, which involved lifting the blockades, after which the JNA units would pull back to major barracks, seemed acceptable.

Having induced Kadijević to put his plan in writing, Wynaendts flew off to Zagreb in the hopes that Tuđman would endorse it. On the way, the EU helicopter was shot at by Croats, but Tuđman attributed the shots to uncontrolled "extremists". When Wynaendts arrived in Zagreb, he was met with the pomp and parade now being daily exhibited in the Croat capital. But when he at last got to Tuđman, the Croat leader "laughed in his face". It was then that Wynaendts sadly recognised that Tuđman, backed by German and Austrian promises of support, now believed that he could get the weapons he needed to go on fighting until he had established control over the whole of what he claimed to be his Croatia.

By August the Troika had lost control of the situation and the EU decided to call on the former British Foreign Secretary, Lord Carrington, to chair a Yugoslav peace conference. This would take over negotiations and Wynaendts was highly impressed by this "gentlemanly" Englishman. He never seemed to appreciate the fact that the Troika's approach was very different from the terms which Carrington favoured. In a series of plans and proposals, Carrington consistently argued that there should be no recognition of the new statelets until agreement had been reached on the security of the Serb communities in Tuđman's Croatia and, later, in Izetbegović's Bosnia. Some form of "special status" should be accorded in the areas where Serbs were a clear majority. In such areas, Serbs should have the right to manage their own affairs and to police themselves. The deal would then be internationally guaranteed. Any agreement would thus need to be endorsed by Serbia as well as Croatia.

The Croat plans fitted into the German resolve to offer the new statelets unconditional recognition. As the EU had clearly got nowhere, the main governments, notably the French, suggested that the responsibilities for endorsing any peace plan should be transferred from the EU to the UN. The Serbs were by now convinced that the EU was their enemy and eagerly supported this shift to New York. General Ratko Mladić, a former member of the JNA and, from July 1991, the commander of the Bosnian Serb army, treated the EU representatives with undisguised scorn. Wynaendts, who met him in March 1992, found him "loud and brutal".

The West too easily believed anti-Yugoslavia claims that the JNA had an overwhelming superiority in arms. It was indeed true that the JNA had more pieces of heavy artillery than the other warring groups. It is also true that, when the international communities forced the JNA to pull out of Bosnia, most of the recruits turned out to be residents of Bosnia and not only refused to leave but held on to their weapons.

But in measuring the respective armed forces, it also has to be taken into account that Tito had concentrated his arms production, reserves of spare parts and reservoirs of oil in the areas around Sarajevo and Mostar. It was the Muslims who dominated this region and this fitted into Tito's known reluctance to place his military-industrial complex in areas controlled by the Serbs. He had good reason to mistrust the loyalty of the Serbs to his own command.

The Croats entered the struggle with forces inferior to those of the JNA, but the German and Austrian backers of the new statelet had no difficulty purchasing plenty of arms, ammunition and equipment from world markets, particularly Eastern Europe. The new material reached Croatia easily with the tacit support of Hungary, and within a very short time the Croats acquired more modern and technically advanced weapons than those available to the JNA.

The JNA's quantity of arms was not matched by quality. On 8 March 1995 the Croat minister of defence derided the value of a lot of the JNA equipment which had fallen into Croat hands after the capture of Krajina. A lot of it, he said, "was antiquated and not worth having." What the Croats did value were the bases and rail communication with Dalmatia which could be restored after the Krajina offensive.

*The Times* correspondent reported on 8 July 1995 that "the Bosnian Muslims and Bosnian Croats, as well as the Serbs, have quite enough weapons to indefinitely sustain the slaughter".

Another underlying misconception, first spelled out by Wynaendts but later commanding the minds of most Western policy-makers, was the assumption that the Muslim leader, Izetbegović, was a moderate. Wynaendts tells us he was impressed by Izetbegović's "serenity" and he manifestly regarded the Muslim leader as a potential friend of a multi-ethnic Bosnia. What he did not know was that Izetbegović and his companions in the newly-formed SDA ruling party, were advocates of pan-Islamic unity. They found their main support not in the West but in the Islamic world. Izetbegović himself was the author of *The Islamic Declaration*, issued first in the underground press in 1970 and again in 1990. In 1990 it appeared openly, and for a brief time was available in Sarajevo news agents. The Western-educated Sarajevo lobby soon saw how much damage it could do, and it is now very hard to find.

*The Declaration* covers some 70 pages and takes a militantly Manichean view of the world. On the one side, Izetbegović lauds the spiritually elevated Islamic world. On the other, he castigates the villainy of governments which have fallen under the corrupting Western influence. Such states include not only those predominantly Christian but also Islamic states which have introduced a secular society.

Izetbegović's supporter, later to become his rival, was Haris Silajdžić. Both men have lived their lives as part of the pan-Islamic world. Though their propaganda gave Westerners the impression of tolerance and open-mindedness, their real friends were the Islamic fundamentalist regimes. Once in power, they put visits to Islamic governments in the Middle East and Asia first. These have consistently agitated to give the Bosnian Muslims military and political support. On 20 September 1992, a pan-Islamic gathering in Zagreb called on all good Muslims to go to Bosnia and fight for the Bosnian Muslim cause.

There was a further issue on which the Troika and Belgrade collided. What remained of Yugoslavia, in practice Serbia and Montenegro, demanded the right to represent the old Yugoslavia in the international community. Wynaendts refused to examine this claim, even though it seemed to be endorsed by international law. As precedents, the Serbs could point out that both India and Russia had been deprived of part of their territory by the secession of component parts. Yet both India and Russia automatically retained the full rights of representation. Belgrade clung unremittingly to the demand that the new Yugoslavia should take up the prerogatives of the old one.

On 13 May 1996, the President of Yugoslavia, Zoran Lilić, declared, yet again, that "nothing was more important than the preservation of the Yugoslav state." But, in deference to Croat and Muslim opinion, the international community stuck to its demand that the new Yugoslavia, with a new constitution, must apply to the international community as if it were a new country. Nonetheless, from the Troika's intervention onward, the Western hostility to the Serbs made it impossible for the leaders of the new Yugoslavia to make themselves heard.

**Footnotes**

1. Wynaendts, Henry (1993). *L'engrenage. Chroniques Yougoslaves Juillet 1991 - Aôut 1992.* Editions Denoel, Paris.

2. Jović, Borislav (1994). *The Last Days of Yugoslavia, Extracts from Diaries.* Belgrade.

3. *Ibid.*

4. *Ibid.*

5. Mesić, Stipe (1994). *How Yugoslavia was Destroyed.* Mislav Press, Zagreb.

6. Marković, Ante. Address to Croatian Assembly, Live relay, Zagreb 0806 gmt, 24 June 1991.

7. A detailed account of the autopsies performed by Dr. Zoran Stanković was published in *Vojnosanitetski Pregled*, 1992.

Slobodan Milošević.
Belgrade. April 1993.

# 3

# Slobodan Milošević — Vicar of Bray

There was once a notorious clergyman in the parish of Bray who changed his creed to suit changes of sovereignty. According to an eighteenth century song, he countered the accusation of being a time server thus: "Not so, neither, for if I changed my religion, I am sure I kept true to my principle, which is to live and die the vicar of Bray." A comparison can be drawn between the careers of Slobodan Milošević and the vicar of Bray. It is Milošević's capacity to concentrate exclusively on his own personal position which has sustained his rule. Such single-mindedness has ruthlessly excluded any principle or any consistency. An awareness of the Serb leader's zig-zagging career is an essential ingredient in understanding the present conflicts.

In a quite unique career, he has managed to switch from a figure of loathing into an indispensable partner in the peace process. How long he can keep his rickety regime in office remains to be seen. But having been in power since 1986, he has already outlasted all of the political leaders, both inside and outside

Yugoslavia, who have been in any way connected with Yugoslav affairs.

A closer look at his record reveals that neither the image of a genocidal villain nor of a willing member of the democratic world was true. He was not the bloodthirsty butcher who haunted Western dreams, nor did he become a Western-orientated democrat determined to Europeanise Serbia. Though he unquestionably contributed to Yugoslavia's downfall, and exacerbated the distrust between the communities, racialism is something of which he could never be accused. The population of Serbia (including Kosovo and Vojvodina) is only 60 percent Serb, the rest is an amalgam of different nationalities against whom Milošević has never displayed hostility.

Both Milošević and his childhood sweetheart, whom he married, came from the little town of Požarevac. He started his life in inauspicious circumstances. By the time he was born in 1941, his mother was already a well-connected member of the Communist Party. She had married a teacher in an Orthodox seminary, but the Party did not approve of such alliances. In 1945 his mother drove his father from their home, and a few years later his father's body was found in Montenegro. It is generally assumed that he killed himself. In 1973 Slobodan's mother died: in this case suicide is certain, though the causes of her desperation were never revealed.

Milošević spent most of his life as a disciplined Party member. While still at the Lycée he joined the Communist Party's Youth League, and by 1983 he had risen to the top level of the Communist Party. His view of his own roots is unclear: he has declared himself a Serb, but his brother has declared himself a Montenegrin.

Milošević's upward strides within the Party *nomenklatura*, which he rapidly climbed, included financial and industrial, as well as political, experience. He spent several months working for a Yugoslav bank in New York and acquired a good enough mastery of the English language to be able to conduct business without an interpreter. Until 1986 he mounted the political ladder under the auspices of his patron and boss, Ivan Stambolić, the son of an eminent Titoist Partisan. In that year, however, Milošević managed not only to discredit his former patron but also to take his place. The occasion for the breach between the two men showed that, by then, Milošević had freed himself from any commitment to Titoism and Titoist ideology.

At issue was the seizure by the communist-controlled police of a memorandum listing Serb grievances against the communist rulers. It had been prepared by a committee and had not been finally edited. Its writers were all members of the Serb Academy of Arts and Science. Stambolić's reactions were predictable. The document, some hundred pages long, was seditiously anti-communist and, according to communist precedent, the writers would have been prosecuted. But Milošević saw things differently. He knew that most Serbs would sympathise with the well-known complaints against the imbecilities and corruption of the "Red Barons", and he daringly cast himself as the willing champion of the revival of Serb national feeling. Nervous Party members sniffed the air and felt that Milošević was a better bet than Stambolić and most of them followed their new leader wherever he led. By now he seemed set to be a main player for life.

The memorandum itself was subsequently seized on by ignorant Western journalists who knew nothing of the background or the reasons for the Serb complaints. Searching for a document which would pinpoint Serb aggressiveness, they claimed that the unfinished memorandum was the Serb equivalent of Hitler's *Mein Kampf*. New arrivals, eager to discover analogies between the present crisis and the last world war, were in search of "written evidence". Yet neither in content nor in style was there the faintest resemblance between Hitler's genocidal blueprint and the doleful memorandum.

In the Serb document the word "genocide" was indeed used, but only to deplore the violence and terror then being used by the Albanian communists, who had been put into power by Tito and his successors. The first time I heard the epithet "ethnic cleansing" was between 1979 and 1984, during my visits to Kosovo. It was the Serbs who were at the receiving end.

For Milošević, 1988 was the real turning point. Having identified himself with Serb national feeling, he went on to address a gathering of Serbs in Priština. On 14 April a large and boisterous Serb crowd had assembled to hear him and the mainly Albanian police took out their truncheons to restore order. This led Milošević to declare: "No one has the right to beat you..." That demonstration of solidarity led many Serbs to regard Milošević as their true champion.

That same year he drew on his communist experience to mobilise "the masses". He visited Vojvodina, Kosovo and Montenegro, and organised rallies designed to drive out the generally corrupt and brutal ruling bureaucracies. These he replaced with men of his own choice. This action gave him nearly, but not quite, enough votes in the collective presidency, which would have enabled him to take a grip on the army.

In May of the same year, 1988, he organised communist-type elections, which were duly boycotted by democratic groupings.

Belgrade's intellectual elite were almost all against him. A critical analysis of the fictive nature of his constitution, which in practice allowed him to do as he liked to whom he liked, was carried out by the expert on international and constitutional law, Kosta Čavoški. Under the title "The Evil Curse of Despotic Government", Čavoški warned that the regime "instills evil and misery into the very foundations of the state" [1].

After subsequent elections, Milošević's parliamentary majority depended, on occasions, on the cooperation of Vojislav Šešelj, the man who favoured using paramilitary units to get rid of non-Serbs in contested areas of Croatia and later, Bosnia. In order to gain favour, Milošević dropped the epithet "communist" in favour of "socialist", a portmanteau word which could cover social democracy. He was then able to say vociferously that he favoured private enterprise.

It was on this "communist" versus "socialist" issue that a collision with his wife, Mira Marković (she never adopted his name), came into the open . Having married when they were very young, Mira had clung to her Marxist-Leninist ideology and went on contributing columns to national newspapers, which articulated the opposition between his views and hers.

In 1990, when the collapse of Yugoslavia seemed imminent, Mira joined the executive of a newly formed League of Communists, which had been set up in order to reassert the control of the Communist-controlled ex-Partisans inside the Yugoslav army. The head of the movement, a Croat, Admiral Mamula, came to London and addressed a very Titoist public at the Royal United Services Institute (RUSI) [2]. He called for them to support his plan to save Yugoslavia by implementing a Titoist / Partisan coup in the Yugoslav army. Relying on Titoist communism to preserve

Yugoslavia seemed a perilous course and the editor of RUSI's journal gave me space for a letter spelling out my foreboding. [3]

Despite their ideological rift, the Milošević / Marković couple went on living together without any hint of extramarital relations. Until 1990 they lived in a small apartment in the middle of Belgrade; later they moved into a well-defended villa in the elegant suburb of Dedinje. This was the area which hosted ambassadors, VIPs and profiteers. It was reported that Milošević's only pleasures outside politics were whisky and gardening.

After taking power in the 1980s, and holding on to it into the 1990s, Milošević did allow his opponents to have limited access to the Serb media. A flurry of anti-communist newspapers and books began to appear in Belgrade and he allowed a local TV station to express opposition views. What he always kept to himself, however, was the all-Serbian TV channel which reached the general public throughout the country. This carried only what he thought his compatriots should be allowed to know.

In the early years of his leadership, Milošević remained highly suspicious of outside intervention. In August 1991 he gave an interview in which he said foreigners were welcome in Yugoslavia "but not foreign soldiers" [4]. He recalled the appalling losses suffered by the Serbs in both world wars and said that, this time, the Yugoslav people must be left free to settle their own differences. He insisted, as he was often to do later, that the Serbs were demanding no more than the right to protect their own homes, and he called for "equal treatment" towards all national groupings. Assuming an American audience, he recalled that Texas would never have allowed the Mexican-inhabited parts of the state to secede and said that all he was demanding was the same rights for the state of Yugoslavia.

Evidence of tensions between Milošević and the Bosnian Serb leaders was already surfacing by 1992. He began warning incredulous foreign negotiators that he could not control the Bosnian Serb leadership. Though few believed him, he was right. The Bosnian Serb leader, Radovan Karadžić, and his supporters were struggling to assert an anti-communist line, and in this they were supported by the Orthodox Church and the majority of the Bosnian Serb electorate. Karadžić, who enjoyed overwhelming support, drew on the traditions of the wartime leader, Draža Mihailović, whereas Milošević identified himself with the Partisans.

These complex internal divisions were unknown to David Owen who, in 1992, had succeeded Lord Carrington as chairman of the Geneva based Conference on Yugoslavia. Owen had set his heart — and staked his reputation — on getting the international community to support his peace plan, which he believed could be imposed on the recalcitrant Serbs by force if necessary. The plan was put forward by himself and Cyrus Vance, who represented the UN. It proposed dividing Bosnia and Hercegovina into ten non-contiguous slabs of territory, but the closer I examined it the less it seemed likely that it could be acceptable to the Bosnian Serbs. One of the slabs allocated to the Bosnian Serbs would have been entirely surrounded by land controlled by the Bosnian Croats or the Bosnian Muslims, with no provision for its defence.

What was surely needed was some alternative deal, and with this in view I accepted an invitation to Belgrade by the then President of the rump Yugoslavia, Dobrica Ćosić. On 15 April 1993, I managed to arrange an interview with Milošević which lasted 90 minutes. He came alone. I was accompanied by my nephew,

Bruno Beloff, who took photographs and taped our talk. Through the whole of our meeting, Milošević was never disturbed, giving the impression that he had nothing much to do. When I took the occasion to deplore his policies, which I felt had isolated and damaged Serbia, he remained amiable but adamant. I could see why he thought it right to offer the diminishing Serb population in Kosovo the security they badly needed. But surely, before military intervention, he should have drawn the attention of international opinion to the desolate and terrorised condition in which, under the Albanian bosses put into power by Tito and his successors, these Serbs had lived?

When we met, international opinion was highly agitated over the future of Srebrenica, then under the command of the Bosnian Muslim leader, Naser Orić. The UNPROFOR commander at the time was the Frenchman, General Morillon, and he had undertaken to disarm and demilitarize the town. In practice this proved too difficult. Orić held on to most of his weapons and he was subsequently to use Srebrenica as a launching pad from which to attack neighbouring Serb villages. The Serb peasants who lived there were either killed or expelled. Milošević told Owen that he would urge the Bosnian Serb leaders to refrain from taking the town. After some hesitation, Srebrenica was left under Orić's control.

Milošević agreed with me that the Vance-Owen "ten-bit" plan was unworkable and that the Bosnian Serbs would never accept it. Both he and the Bosnian Serb leaders favoured renegotiating the territorial settlement: in return for acquiring parts of Sarajevo, the Muslims would have to give up the Drina enclaves —

Srebrenica, Žepa and Goražde. But the Muslim leaders, encouraged by the Americans, rejected any kind of compromise.

At an EC meeting in Greece, Karadžić, under pressure from Milošević and the Greeks, signed the Vance-Owen Plan but added the proviso that it would only be implemented if endorsed by the Pale Assembly representing the Bosnian Serbs. Encouraged by General Mladić, the Assembly rejected the plan and the whole Vance-Owen operation collapsed. In reality, the Izetbegović-led Sarajevo government also opposed the plan and the only group which enthusiastically endorsed it were the Bosnian Croats. In this, they were fully supported by the Croat government in Zagreb.

The Croats took up positions to which, under the Vance-Owen Plan, they would have been entitled, but the Bosnian Muslims rejected the deal and mobilised their own force to try and drive the Croats back. A bitter Muslim / Croat war ensued which lasted almost a year and in which there were far more casualties than in the preceding Serb / Croat conflict. David Owen has emphatically denied that the Vance-Owen Plan set the scene for the Muslim / Croat conflict, but the record belies him.

In February 1993 the Americans forced the Croats and Muslims to end their conflict and join forces against the Serbs. Rearmed Croats and Muslims took the military offensive. In 1995 they were backed by air strikes from American-led forces, based on aircraft carriers stationed in the Adriatic. Though the Bosnian Serbs were on the defensive, the international community, led by the Americans and the Germans, continued to treat them as "the aggressors". In May 1992 the United Nations Security Council (UNSC) had already imposed sanctions against Serbia which, in their severity, exceeded any punitive measures that the council had ever previously enforced. Contacts with the Serbs of Serbia were prohibited, not only in economic and diplomatic relations, but also in sport and between intellectuals.

When first imposed, these measures consolidated Milošević's authority. All the sufferings of the Serb population, most of it due to his own maladministration, could be blamed on international enmity. Many of his former critics felt this was no time to rock the boat. Further, Milošević's policy offered his people what most of them wanted: assurances that Serbia would not be dragged into war and that its people could be free to turn their minds to non-military matters.

Nonetheless, the sanctions increasingly deprived ordinary Serbs of necessary nourishment and health. Just how damaging the sanctions became was revealed in the summer of 1995 by *Time* magazine [5]. Manifestly basing its evidence on Western sources, *Time* declared that a third of the Serbian labour force was unemployed and that the country's GNP had halved since sanctions had come into effect. The magazine reported that an estimated two million of the ten million population lived "below the poverty line". Predictably it was children and old people who were the principal victims.

For black marketeers, of course, the imposition of sanctions had been welcome. A large amount of hard currency had entered Serbia, and permitted the import of luxuries, but these were available only to illegal traffickers. Competing mafiosi virtually took over the Serb economy and Milošević could do little about it.

Against this chaotic background, Milošević never lost sight of his task of trying to get rid of Karadžić, his principal Serb enemy. In the spring of 1996 the outside negotiators, led by Carl Bildt, tried to have Karadžić replaced by Rajko Kasagić, whom Karadžić had previously named as his prime minister. Kasagić turned out to be more docile and accommodating to the West than Karadžić's other supporters and was dismissed. Milošević immediately backed international efforts to support Kasagić and echoed the Western negotiators in declaring that Kasagić's dismissal had been illegal and invalid. This particular manoeuvre backfired: Kasagić, after trying to play an independent role, had to accept that he had no following and he quietly abandoned his efforts to offer an alternative political option.

Meanwhile, Milošević was being rewarded for his docility. In May 1996 the NATO military commanders called on him in Belgrade, as did the German Foreign Minister, Klaus Kinkel. Wiping from his mind all the protests he had made against the evil consequences of German policy towards Yugoslavia, he welcomed Kinkel as a long-lost, much-loved colleague. He told Kinkel that he was ready to take back some 120,000 refugees who had been seeking political asylum in Germany [6]. The Germans made no objection to his demand that the two "entities", set up by the international community, would enjoy equal treatment. In return, Kinkel recalled German eagerness to restore the activities of German banks and businesses in Serbia. Even during the harshest sanctions, these had never been truly ruptured. Major German firms had quietly continued to install utilities in Serbia as before and to do business in Serbian cities.

Milošević could also now count on Boris Yeltsin's backing. At first, Moscow had veered between Belgrade and the Bosnian Serbs, but by the autumn of 1994 the Russians came down firmly on Milošević's side and helped reopen the Sarajevo airport, from then on under UNPROFOR control. Milošević also made special efforts to cooperate closely with Yasushi Akashi, the Japanese head of the UNSC negotiating team. When, in retaliation to the NATO air strikes, the Bosnian Serbs captured UNPROFOR hostages, Milošević made sure that their release would take place inside Serbia and under his personal management.

In itself none of this international backing guaranteed that Milošević would preserve his power. Serbia is manifestly divided. The economy has slipped out of his control and the country is overrun by hundreds of thousands of angry and vociferous refugees, who strongly disapprove of Milošević's apparent indifference to their suffering. Many of them hold him responsible for allowing the Tuđman forces to capture Western Slavonia in 1994 and Krajina in the summer of 1995. This was done with Ustasha-style violence. Over 150,000 Serbs were driven out from Krajina alone, and many were killed or tortured along the way. None of this prevented Milošević from retaining friendly relations with the Croat president, Franjo Tuđman, to whom the capture of Krajina was a matter of pride.

However things now go, Milošević has already demonstrated how a single politician can defy the world and hold on to office. He has thought, first and foremost, about how best to shore up his power and how to destroy his enemies. And, like the Vicar of Bray, he has so far succeeded.

**Footnotes**

1. Čavoški, Kosta (1996). Evil Curse of Despotic Government, *The South Slav Journal*, Volume 17 No. 1-2 (63-64).

2. Admiral Mamula (1991). *RUSI Journal*, Vol. 136, No. 1.

3. Beloff, Nora. *Ibid*.

4. Milošević, Slobodan. Interview on B Sky B Television, 7 August 1991.

5. *Time*, 17 July 1995.

6. Deutschlandfunk Radio, 16 May 1996.

Muslim refugee and Serb refugee, both from Sarajevo.
Pančevo, Serbia. 27 January 1994.

# 4

# Kosovo — The Insoluble Dilemma

According to the map bequeathed by Tito, Kosovo remained part of Serbia. But from 1974 it was ruled not from Belgrade but by Albanian communists in Priština. There is still a widespread illusion that, under the communists, Kosovo enjoyed "Autonomy". But if autonomy means being ruled by a government controlled by the residents, that was never true. Those who controlled local power and patronage were selected not by the local electorate but by the Communist Party.

The mythology of Kosovo "Autonomy" was boosted by the Croats and Slovenes while they were preparing to declare their own independence. Though the secessionist leaders were not themselves communist, it served as a useful diversion from Yugoslavia's impending collapse. The belief that Kosovo had enjoyed autonomy was widely accepted and became the politically correct opinion in most of the Western world.

In reality there is no tidy solution to the problem of Kosovo. An analogy here could be drawn from Ulster: however much political luminaries try to articulate compromise, there is no device which can satisfy both those who wish to keep Ulster part of the UK and those who see the same territory as part of the Republic of Ireland. A similar incompatibility makes it hopeless to please those who see Kosovo as part of Yugoslavia and the politically active secessionists who see Kosovo as an independent republic, with freedom to merge into a Greater Albania.

The Albanians are the most numerous of Yugoslavia's non-Slav minorities. Ethnically and linguistically they are quite distinct from any other group. According to the 1971 census, they accounted for about six percent of Yugoslavia's population. But the Albanians are not concentrated in Kosovo — or as it is more correctly called, Kosovo-Metohija, the second epithet denoting land that had belonged to the Church. Equal numbers of Albanians are scattered between the other federal entities: Serbia, Montenegro and Macedonia. The official census in Macedonia has been challenged by the Albanians, who claim to represent as much as 30 percent of its population. Albanian activists in Macedonia have stolidly refused to recognise the legitimacy of the present Macedonian government.

The struggle for the contested territory of Kosovo between Christians and Muslims has lasted for many centuries. Neither of the communities has felt safe unless they have populated the region with their own nationals. Unjustly, the rest of Europe is inclined to pick up on this corner of Europe as particularly savage and genocidal. Yet the record of Central and Eastern Europe is no better. It is useful to recall that in these regions after the last war, there were some 12 million refugees and displaced persons seeking asylum, and many irredentist claims still survive.

Confronted with any insoluble problem, it is the custom of diplomats to by-pass the deadlock by use of double-talk, so making it seem that they are giving each community what it wants. This double-talk has featured prominently in the discussion on Ulster. On Kosovo, foreign diplomats seem both to support the pro-Albanian lobby under its secessionist leader, Ibrahim Rugova, yet, at the very same time, declare that there can be no change of frontiers: the province of Kosovo must be satisfied with autonomy. This they wrongly see as a return to the previous arrangement. But the people of Kosovo had never had autonomy, if autonomy means the right to select their own leadership.

To understand the complexities we need to go centuries back. The Serbs had settled in Kosovo in the early Middle Ages, and it was in Kosovo that the first Serbian kingdom was based. During that time the Albanians were barely two percent of the Kosovo population and consisted mainly of shepherds living in the mountains. In the fourteenth and fifteenth centuries, the Ottomans conquered the whole area and the Serbs began migrating north or west. Migrations, sometimes ordered by the Turks and sometimes from fear of reprisals, primarily to Krajina and Slavonia, the border regions of the Hapsburg Empire, took place in the sixteenth and seventeenth centuries, when the Austrians invited the Serbs to settle. In return for land and security, these agreed to fight to defend the Empire against Turkish assaults. Until the beginning of the eighteenth century, the Serbs remained a majority in Kosovo. Subsequently, the Ottoman rulers sent in Islamised Albanian settlers to secure the region [1].

By the eighteenth century the Turkish Empire started weakening. The Congress of Berlin in 1878 allowed Austria to occupy Bosnia and Hercegovina to provide stability in the region. In 1908 Austria unilaterally annexed Bosnia and Hercegovina, without seeking the approval of the other Great Powers. The Turks, feeling on the defensive, practised a policy of persecution. They saw the Christians as dangerous enemies and many thousands were exterminated. It was during this period that the Serbs, many of whom fled, were reduced to a minority in Kosovo, which they have remained ever since. During the Second World War the Axis allocated Kosovo to a Greater Albania, which became a protectorate of Italy.

At the end of the War, Tito was resolved to secure Kosovo for his Yugoslavia and sent in Partisans, who, after thousands of casualties (the number has never been revealed), asserted Tito's authority. At first he entrusted Kosovo to his police chief, Alexander Ranković, who was as brutal to the members of the Orthodox Church as he was to the Muslim and Christian clergymen.

But Tito, as we have seen, distrusted the Serbs and did not want Kosovo to become a beacon of Serb nationalism. Many Serbs had fled during the war and he prohibited any of them from returning. He also confiscated the land and property they owned in Kosovo. It was after the student disturbances of 1968 that he changed course. Hoping to exercise stronger control, he shifted power and patronage from the Belgrade communists to locally recruited Kosovo Albanians. He and his successors recruited only those Kosovo Albanians known to be loyal to them. He gave these trustees freedom to build up local support and to revenge themselves on their hereditary enemies: the Serbs. Justifiably, the Serbs accused the Kosovo Albanians of practising "ethnic cleansing" to rid villages of Serb families.

To avoid internal turbulence after the communist Albanians took power, Tito prohibited the Serbian media from reporting what was happening in Kosovo. It was a form of censorship which his successors managed to maintain for several years after his death. Nonetheless, news percolated through and it was pent up Serb indignation about events in Kosovo which the Serbian leader, Slobodan Milošević, exploited to build up enthusiasm for himself. Within a few months in 1987, his image was transformed from a regular member of the communist *nomenklatura* (in which he made his name) into what many Serbs saw as a champion of Serb survival. By sending in the Yugoslav army, the Serbs felt he was defending his battered people against Albanian persecution.

Life had become increasingly insecure for the rapidly diminished Serb population, whom the Albanians were resolved to drive out of Kosovo. Between 1979 and 1984, while I was collecting material for my last book [2], I visited Kosovo several times and saw for myself that the Serbs still living in Kosovo were harassed and terrified, and had no recourse to legal protection for themselves or their families.

My first visit to Priština, the capital, was brief. I went there in 1979 and, without warning, all foreigners were summarily expelled as part of the security measures preceding a visit from Tito. By the time he arrived he was already a very sick man and spoke pessimistically of the future of Yugoslavia. This was his last visit to Kosovo. A year later he died in Ljubljana, having been comatose for many months.

Testimony on the persecution of the Serbs in the 1980s is available from the internationally recognised forensic scientist, Dr. Zoran Stanković. He told me that in 1983, he was attached to a military unit in Kosovo, but did not need much time to look after the soldiers, and so offered his services to the local population, Serb and Albanian alike. The Kosovo Albanians were so pleased that he was willing to look after their families that they told him that, whatever happened in Kosovo, he and his wife and children would be safe. They gave him to understand that they planned to assault and, if possible, to expel other Serbs, but would make him an exception. So Dr. Stanković found himself looking after both Albanians and their Serb victims. Methods used to terrorise the

Serbs into leaving included raping Serbian women, and Dr. Stanković did what he could to give these medical assistance.

Conditions in Kosovo today can have no international parallel. The disparity in numbers made it impossible for the mainly Serb military units to control the country and they have made no attempt to interfere with the use of the Albanian language in schools and colleges. Some 20 Albanian language newspapers, many highly critical of the Serbs, are allowed to appear. What is still more remarkable is that the Albanians, under the secessionist leader, Ibrahim Rugova, have been free to organise a parallel structure of government, going all the way from "President" Rugova himself, who lived within 50 metres of the Serb HQ in Priština, down to local administration and the management of the smallest teaching unit. The Albanian secessionists have so far stuck mainly to passive resistance and the Serbs have let them have their way.

Though Kosovo remains undeveloped and belongs more to the Third World than to Europe, there has been no shortage of money. On the official side, Kosovo has been the principal beneficiary of the Yugoslav development fund which, under the Titoist system, was paid by the northern provinces to the south. There was also a regular input of funds to Kosovo from the World Bank and other international providers. The trouble, as in so much of the Third World, was that the money went to local rulers and there was no effective accountability on how it was spent. At a symposium at Oxford in 1983, one International Monetary Fund (IMF) official said that the money allocated to Kosovo just "disappeared into a black hole."

Rugova's parallel institutions were also flush with money. Large numbers of Kosovo Albanians had emigrated to the West and many were involved in drug trafficking. It was widely known that the buying and selling of drugs was Rugova's secessionists' principal asset. Though this was known to the outside world, most diplomats did not want to damage relations with Kosovo's parallel government.

International double-talk has encouraged the secessionists to hope that turbulence in Kosovo may induce Western powers to take a more benevolent view of secessionist aims. Small scale acts of violence can be relied on to bring Kosovo back into the newspapers, and many Westerners now believe that there can be no solution to the problems of ex-Yugoslavia without some changes in Kosovo's status.

In February 1996 the British Foreign Minister, Malcolm Rifkind, visited Tirana and, while there, received Rugova and discussed Kosovo's future. I wrote to him pointing out that Rugova's stated ambition was an independent Kosovo, and by receiving the secessionist leader in a foreign capital Rifkind was surely encouraging a prospect which countered official Western policy: to preserve Kosovo as part of Serbia. FCO officials wrote to me several times insisting that our basic policy had not changed and that all we demanded was that the Serbs grant more "autonomy" to the Kosovo Albanians. The writers seemed not to know that the Serbs had repeatedly offered the Kosovo Albanians freedom to manage their own affairs but that Rugova's supporters were unwilling to discuss anything less than independence.

The Americans gave a further boost to Rugova's aspirations by installing their own special office in Priština. The Rugova people joyously interpreted this as an official mission from Washington to their parallel government.

Outside intervention has only made things worse. Foreign diplomats should leave the Serbs and Albanians to work out their own form of coexistence in Kosovo. There are phases of small-scale violence, in which two or three Serbs are killed by Albanians or two or three Albanians by Serbs. Such skirmishes, when they reach the Western press, tend to be played up as signifying an approaching apocalypse.

The trouble in Kosovo started hundreds of years before the present conflict in ex-Yugoslavia and will no doubt last several hundred years after this conflict is forgotten. It would be quite wrong to insist, as many do-gooders are inclined to do, that the Yugoslav conflict cannot end without "resolving" the Kosovo troubles. It was not the Kosovo Albanians, nor the Serbs, who were responsible for the death of Yugoslavia. The assassins were a group of extremist Croats, the subject of the next chapter.

**Footnotes**

1. Bogdanović, Dimitrije (1985). *Knjiga o Kosovu* [*The Book of Kosovo*]. Serbian Academy of Sciences and Arts.

2. Beloff, Nora (1985). *Tito's Flawed Legacy*. Gollancz.

Spanish UNPROFOR soldier, Bosnian Muslim soldier and civilians
waiting for returning POWs.

East Mostar, Bosnia and Hercegovina. 20 March 1994.

# 5

# How Franjo Tuđman and his Ustasha Backers Managed Yugoslavia's Collapse

Two dominant factors marked the collapse of Yugoslavia. First, the election of Franjo Tuđman, with a small lead on a low turnout, who won on the racialist platform "Croatia for the Croats" — implying little or no room for anyone else. Second, Tuđman derived money and manpower from the Ustasha, a party which had supported the Nazis during the Second World War. The survivors subsequently fled overseas, where they set up powerful lobbies, particularly in Latin America, the USA, Australia and New Zealand.

Tuđman urged the Ustasha and their descendants to return and replace the non-Croats residing in what he claimed was his Croatia. (This included a slab of what was, in 1992, internationally recognised as Bosnia and Hercegovina. It was on the Hercegovina border that the Ustasha had been particularly strong).

The exodus of Serbs started as soon as Tuđman was elected. When I visited Croatia soon afterwards, I could see that the Serbs had good reasons to be afraid. Serbs living among Croats were victims of arson, beatings and expropriation, and could expect no justice from Tuđman's courts. Individual Serbs, whose names had been printed on "death lists" published in Croat newspapers, were often kidnapped and presumed killed [1].

The exodus reached its peak in 1994 and 1995 when Tuđman's forces overran the regions of Western Slavonia and Krajina. They expelled or killed the mainly peasant Serb population. Most houses were destroyed but those left standing were offered to any Ustasha family wishing to come home to Croatia, and to Croatian refugees from Bosnia.

The Partisans were a mixed bunch and Tuđman, though always a racialist, served in their ranks as an officer and, after the War, became Tito's youngest general. He was promoted by the Communist Party to become the Partisan's official historian. A German socialist, Eberhard Dingel, recently recalled visiting Zagreb as part of a "fraternal delegation" and being amazed to find Tuđman, though wearing a Partisan uniform, feeling free to express overt anti-Semitism [2].

It was not until 1986 that Tuđman sacrificed his array of well-paid party jobs and perks. He was expelled from the party when he publicly linked himself to the nationalist cause. The occasion was his signature of a collective letter denouncing the "Serbianisation" of the Croat language. His dedication to what he conceived as linguistic purity subsequently led him to restore archaic forms of expression and, where necessary, to invent new words, rather than use the vocabulary current in Serbia. Today, Tuđman's own writing is often incomprehensible, not only to most of Yugoslavia, but also to Croat intellectuals.

With a well trained lobby, Tuđman and his Ustasha backers knew they needed Western support and they did their best to present themselves as part of the European family. In his first government Tuđman even named a well known economist, Dražen

Kalodjera, to be his "minister for privatisation". Within weeks, Kalodjera resigned, having discovered that Tuđman intended to tighten rather than loosen his grip on the national assets.

In view of his Ustasha connections, it might seem strange that Tuđman was so successful in selling himself to Western leaders. Here, the British took the lead. In the mood of post-communist euphoria, the Conservative Party invited Tuđman to London in May, 1991, and his lecture [3], plainly put together by Western-trained aides, told the Tories just what they wanted to hear. Tuđman was introduced to the then Prime Minister, Margaret Thatcher, who promptly declared him "one of us". In subsequent years both Mrs. Thatcher and the Foreign Office went on backing the Croats and denouncing the Serbs. When I once asked her why, she replied briefly that she would always defend a democrat (meaning Tuđman) against a communist (meaning Milošević).

The pro-Tuđman tradition was well-established when, on the celebration of the fiftieth anniversary of the allied victory in Europe, the Foreign Secretary, Douglas Hurd, placed the Croat leader on his right at a dinner in London. There was no representative from the Serbs of Yugoslavia regardless of the fact that these, unlike the Ustasha, had been on the Western side during the War.

On his home ground, Tuđman made no effort to conceal his close involvement with the Ustasha and his belief that he was reviving the independent state of Croatia, installed by the Nazis during the War. The chequered flag of the Ustasha was the official emblem. The currency, the Kuna, took the name it had had during the War and "U" for Ustasha was painted prominently in all the areas which the Croats captured.

There has been some dispute about whether fascism as an ideology is now a thing of the past. In *The Sunday Times* [4] I argued that, on the contrary, Tuđman's regime had all the trappings of fascism: racialism, militarism, a passion for uniforms, the cult of the leader and a corporatist control of the economy.

The worst of the Ustasha's wartime atrocities were carried out in the concentration camp of Jasenovac, where hundreds of thousands of Serbs, Jews and Gypsies were shot or hacked to death. Tuđman knocked a nought off the numbers believed to have been killed and claimed that the beneficiaries had been the Jews who had served as wardens and administrators. Unsurprisingly, no Israeli knowing this background will shake hands with the Croat leader. Tuđman has also announced that the site of the concentration camp will be turned into a park and memorial for all the victims of the last War. In other words, the Ustasha will be buried and honoured together with their victims.

It remains doubtful whether Tuđman would have unilaterally declared independence, as he did on 25th June 1991, had he not been challenged to do so by the more militantly nationalist, ex-communist Slovene leader, Milan Kučan. Like so many other former communist *apparatchiks*, Kučan espoused the nationalist cause in the hopes of living down his previous record. Outwardly, there seemed little cause for Slovene discontent with its participation in Yugoslavia. Its industrialisation had already started before Yugoslavia was created and, within the Yugoslav protectionist economy, it had a captive market for its manufactures. Thus, while the rest of Europe suffered from unemployment, Slovenia's trouble was labour shortage.

Nor, in recent times, have the Slovenes suffered any form of repression. In practice, they had run their own affairs since 1974, and nationalist feelings were freely and passionately expressed. Tension between Ljubljana and Belgrade sharpened in 1989 when the Yugoslav Peoples' Army prosecuted a group of young

Slovenes, led by the secessionists' champion, Janez Janša. They were charged with having published a secret report and a brief jail sentence only enhanced the image of the young revolutionaries.

Relations went from bad to worse. After Yugoslav military units had been sent into Kosovo, the Slovenes loudly sided with the Kosovo Albanians. The Serbs retaliated by organising a boycott of Slovene products and the Slovenes responded by suspending payments into the federal budget. Then, in 1990, the Slovene Assembly declared that, from then on, Slovene laws would take precedence over federal laws and that Slovene conscripts would not serve in the federal army outside Slovenia. Predictably, the federal constitutional court declared these decisions invalid and, equally predictably, the Slovenes took no notice.

In January 1991, Kučan announced that within six months Slovenia would secede from Yugoslavia, and when time was up he took the dramatic step of sending Slovene policemen to haul down the Yugoslav flags along the Austrian frontier. The Slovenes then proceeded to help themselves to the customs revenues collected at the frontier, on which the federal government heavily depended.

In Belgrade, this challenge found the Yugoslav Peoples' Army divided and unsure of its next step. After trying in vain to intimidate Ljubljana by a dispatch of heavy vehicles and aircraft, Belgrade decided to send in 3,000 conscripts. Their task was to restore the Yugoslav flag and, as no resistance was expected, the men were not even given anti-flak protection. Most of them had no idea of what they were expected to do. This wretched little force gave the Slovene nationalists the "War of Independence" which they needed. It lasted 10 days, provided excellent TV images and cost the lives of 19 Slovenes and 45 federal soldiers.

Though the Slovene action was manifestly in defiance of the Helsinki Final Act, which precluded changes of frontiers in Europe, the Slovenes had no difficulty in mobilising Western opinion on their side. At this juncture Tudman could hardly show himself to have been upstaged. Having ruptured relations with the rest of Yugoslavia, he declared that the units of the federal army stationed in his Croatia, of which there were a large number, must either surrender or be deprived of food, light and communications with the outside world. War had begun.

**Footnotes**

1. After a fact finding mission in Croatia, Marijana Grandits, a member of the Austrian Parliament, stated that " ... authorities took no action even in cases when Serbs were murdered. The MP believes that in Croatia a 'subtle form of ethnic cleansing is taking place' in order to drive away the Serbs. (Vienna's *Der Standard*, 5/6 September 1992). Ivan Čičak, head of the Croatian Helsinki Watch, stated : "Since 1991 the Croatian authorities have blown up or razed 10,000 houses, mostly of Serbs ... " According to Čičak 280,000 Croatian Serbs had fled; of Zagreb's 60,000 Serbs, 20,000 remained. (*The New York Times*, 8 December 1993).

2. Eberhard Dingel in conversation with Nora Beloff, 1993.

3. Tuđman, Franjo (1991). *Croatia at the Crossroads in Search of a Democratic Confederacy*. Centre for Policy Studies, London.

4. Beloff, Nora (6 August 1995). *The Sunday Times*, Letters.

Bosnian Serb sniper.

Near Grbavica, Republika Srpska. 10 May 1994.

# 6

# Germany's Dominant Role

In the short term, the initiators of Yugoslavia's collapse were Franjo Tuđman and his Ustasha collaborators. But they would never have succeeded without German and Austrian backing. On the subject of ex-Yugoslavia, there is no point in treating Germany and Austria separately. It was Germany's intervention against Yugoslavia that set the scene for the current conflicts.

The heir to the former Austro-Hungarian Empire, Otto von Habsburg, has without compunction had himself naturalised German and now sits in the European Assembly, representing a Bavarian constituency. He has been actively engaged in propagating the case for military intervention against Serbia.

The present conflict and, more particularly, the extraordinary flight of hundreds of thousands of Serbs out of Croatia, cannot be understood without examining Germany's record in World War Two. In March 1941, Hitler had supposed that he had managed to bribe and bully the Yugoslav leader, Prince Paul, into joining the Axis powers. His plans were thwarted by a mutiny led by Serbian officers which deposed the Prince Regent and replaced him with the 17 year-old King Peter. Hitler flew into a rage which is described in lurid detail in the daily diary of his minister, Josef Goebbels [1]. Hitler resolved that the Serbs, along with the Jews and Gypsies, would rank among the peoples to be destroyed. The new Belgrade government tried to reassure the Germans, but to no avail. Goebbels gave his interpretation of the climb down by the new Yugoslav government:

"They are shitting themselves in Belgrade... The provocation will be avenged and they probably realise it. They are being so mild and co-operative that this has the ring of panic in it..."

The blitz began with an air raid on Belgrade, which cost 26,000 lives. Joachim von Ribbentrop, then Hitler's Foreign Minister, made himself responsible for implementing Hitler's anti-Serb policy and, for this purpose, brought Ante Pavelić back to Zagreb. Pavelić was leader of a far right marginal group with a genocidal anti-Serb programme. He and his colleagues, who had represented only a small minority in Croatia, had fled from Yugoslavia and placed themselves under Mussolini's protection.

The record shows that the Nazi leaders themselves were divided about the wisdom of Ribbentrop's choice. Some were later to complain that Pavelić's excesses made Yugoslavia's territories much harder to govern. Nonetheless, there was no effective opposition and Pavelić remained in office until the Germans were defeated. In carrying through this holocaust against the Serbs, the Ustasha were fully supported by the German army. We have the well-documented account of Germany's military responsibility in Jonathan Steinberg's book *All or Nothing: the Axis and the Holocaust 1941-1943* [2]. Taking his evidence from military archives, Steinberg concluded that, whereas the Italian officers did their best to oppose genocidal orders from their political chiefs, the Germans fell obediently into line.

The Germans, being busy preparing their assault on the USSR, limited themselves in Yugoslavia to occupying the main lines of communication. In order to protect their army, the Germans resorted to a policy of massive retaliation: 100 Serb civilians would be executed publicly for every German soldier killed, and 50 for every German wounded. In the vicinity of the town of Kragujevac, several German soldiers had been killed, and as there were not enough hostages in the prisons, the Germans rounded up the town's male population. To make up the numbers, they also shot 300 boys and 18 teachers from the local high school. It was these memories, handed down over generations, that inflamed Serb terror of the Germans. German public opinion, forgetful of events so long ago, retaliated by treating the modern Serbs as barbarians.

There can be no doubt that the solid support of German and Austrian opinion constituted a major factor in inciting the Slovene and Croatian secessionists to risk rupture. The policy of the German government lagged behind German public opinion. The German media was overwhelmingly pro-Croat and pro-Catholic, and the public, viewing anti-Serb TV soundbites, demanded action.

The German Foreign Minister, Hans Deitrich Genscher, was reluctant to break with other Europeans. He would have preferred to preserve the status quo. He had been in international affairs long enough to have worked on friendly terms with the last Yugoslav Foreign Minister, Budimir Lončar, and he resented outside pressure forcing him to back the secessionists.

Genscher was himself a member of the Liberal Party, the junior partner in Chancellor Kohl's coalition government. Though under considerable Catholic pressure, he was not himself a member of the Catholic Church. According to those who worked in the Balkan section of the German Foreign Ministry, the principal pressure came from the newspaper *Frankfurter Allgemeine Zeitung*, which hurled abuse at Genscher for being so slow to recognise the secessionist states. The staff of the Foreign Ministry would refer to the paper as the *Zagreb Allgemeine Zeitung*.

The emergence of the secessionists in the summer of 1991 coincided with negotiations on the Maastricht Treaty. There was a general feeling that the time had now come for the burgeoning European Community to demonstrate its ability to follow common defence policies and to impose a new order in Europe. It is no exaggeration to say that if the European Union had turned its back on Yugoslavia, and let the Yugoslav peoples sort out their own affairs, there would have been neither the subsequent violence nor the exodus of refugees.

One of those closely involved in the negotiations was Henry Wynaendts. In his account [3], two facts emerge which confirm the judgement of other witnesses. First, the Yugoslav Federal Army, left to itself, would have been quite strong enough to have held the secessionists in check. As Wynaendts shows, this was prevented by the determination of over-ambitious European activists "to refuse a *fait accompli*". They never stopped to reflect that all the frontiers of Europe have been created by an acceptance of *fait accompli*.

The second feature emerging from Wynaendts' account is that Yugoslavia was never treated as a problem in its own right. Instead, it was seen as a splendid opportunity to demonstrate the authority of the New Europe. Strutting across the international scene, the representatives of this "New Europe" assumed that they had the right to take control out of the hands of the communities living in Yugoslavia and to impose a new order of their own.

Europe, however, was divided and uncertain, and showed itself quite incapable of imposing alternative rules and systems. Under the European Union's rules of rotation, initiatives had to be taken by a "Troika" consisting of the Foreign Ministers from the countries in whose turn it was to lead, to have led, and to be about to lead the Union. In the Yugoslav case, this produced the Foreign Ministers of Holland, Portugal and Luxembourg, none of whom had any knowledge or experience of the complexities of the Yugoslav crisis.

They so misunderstood the background that they accepted that Tito's final constitution left Yugoslavia with a "Federal Government." As I have indicated, from 1974 onwards the federal government had been virtually paralysed in favour of the separatist forces.

When Wynaendts came into the picture he already shared with his German colleagues an assumption that the repeated failure of European Union initiatives must be the fault of the Serbs, notably Slobodan Milošević. Oddly, this collides with Wynaendts' own detailed reports of events, which show that it was Tuđman, not Milošević, who insisted on the war options.

What had happened was that once Tuđman had determined to take the plunge and declare secession, he confronted the problem of the presence of a Yugoslav Peoples' Army, much of it stationed in what he claimed was his Croatia. In the negotiations with the Europeans, Tuđman frequently promised not to use violence, but in defiance of these pledges he ordered the Croat National Guard (in practice a secessionist army) to blockade and starve out any unit of the Yugoslav Peoples' Army which refused to surrender to Croat forces. Wynaendts freely concedes that Tuđman broke his engagements several times over and tells us that, in the negotiations, the Croat leader habitually blamed "uncontrollable extremists" instead of his own troops. Yet it was the latter who were guilty of disrupting peace negotiations.

The European Union threw all its authority into demanding that on no account should Belgrade use the federal army to save Yugoslavia. General Veljko Kadijević, who was in charge of the Yugoslav army in the summer of 1991, did not dare thwart the outside world. He proposed a deal: if the Croats would demobilise what they called their National Guard, he, in return, would withdraw the Yugoslav Army units to agreed locations. The offer impressed Wynaendts, who got it in writing and then flew to Zagreb to propose it to Tudman, who rejected it.

After a series of meetings, in which a number of ceasefires were agreed and the deals then promptly broken, the European Union decided to call on the former British Foreign Secretary, Lord Carrington, to chair a peace conference. Wynaendts speaks admiringly of Carrington and gives the details of Carrington's peace plan, delivered in October 1991. This would have made the recognition of the independence of Slovenia and Croatia strictly conditional: to qualify, they would have to subscribe to internationally monitored commitments to respect the individual and collective rights of minorities.

Instead, the Germans insisted on unconditional recognition of secession. Carrington has repeatedly said that it was the Germans who frustrated his own project. When, three months later, Carrington's proposals for Bosnia and Hercegovina were rejected by the Americans, he gave up and was succeeded by David Owen, the choice of Owen's friend, Cyrus Vance. By then, Vance, a former Secretary of State, had been appointed the representative of the United Nations for Yugoslavia.

According to Wynaendts, the Germans first put forward, privately, the case for unconditional recognition as early as August

1991. They did so again in October, this time with the support of the Italians and of emissaries of the Vatican. But it was not until December, after the signing of the Maastricht Treaty, that Genscher decided that the time had come to impose a German lead on the wobbly European Community.

In November Genscher announced that, regardless of their partners, the Germans would recognise the secessionist states of Slovenia and Croatia before the end of the year. The challenge came at a time when the British were in no position to object. They needed German support for concessions on the "opt-out" clauses, which enabled Britain to refuse to apply some clauses of the Maastricht agreement. Though the then Foreign Secretary, Douglas Hurd, has denied any linkage, virtually all the others who participated in the talks confirmed that a deal was done in December 1991. The British told the Germans that in return for German support on the desired "opt-out", the Germans could count on British support for their Yugoslav policy.

The Germans had more trouble satisfying the French President, François Mitterrand, who was strongly attached to the French pro-Serb tradition. For several months, as reported in the book by Daniel Vernet [4], Diplomatic Editor of *Le Monde*, relations between Paris and Bonn were painfully tense. Early in 1992, however, Mitterrand gave in. He based his concept of a united Europe on the solidarity of the Franco-German axis, and to this he felt he had to give absolute priority.

In March 1992 I went to Germany and found the German establishment more divided than was generally assumed. There were ferocious arguments both on the future of the European Union and on whether or not the Germans should send troops into Yugoslavia. The link between Tuđman and the wartime Ustasha was widely known and, as I learnt later, the then

President of Germany, Richard von Weisacker, never agreed to receive the Croat leader. Nonetheless, most Germans took a strongly anti-Serb line. When, in 1995, the German author Peter Handke protested that the news in the German media was biased and sensationalist, many denounced him as a defender of genocide.

Could the Germans be induced to reassess their anti-Serb stance? I suggested an article to the liberal newspaper, *Die Zeit*. My old friend Baroness Marion Dornhoff at first rejected this offer on the grounds that *Die Zeit* had its own correspondents in Yugoslavia and these would be offended if the paper published my dissenting view. Further correspondence, however, had more positive results, and in July 1992 I was offered space for a 700 word piece on *Die Zeit*'s leader-page. In it, I concluded that the Western powers should be promoting reconciliation between the warring groups. This would have meant abandoning the policy of confrontation which was "leading, it would seem, to perpetual civil war."

Aiming at more specialist German opinion, I was pleased to receive approval from the German Institute of International Affairs for a 4,000 word study, placing the Yugoslav crisis within its historical context. The staff member Dr. Joachim Thies, who commissioned the piece, was also editor of the Institute's journal *Europe Archiv*. The article I wrote focused primarily on Germany's own responsibility for the current violence, ending:

"The restoration of peace depends first and foremost on a reconciliation between Croats and Serbs in which neither would be humiliated and in which the blame would be fairly shared. Perhaps a change of German Foreign Minister will lead to a more balanced policy." Dr. Thies turned down the piece as too polemical for his journal. My offer of working with him to find a more suitable style was ignored.

In predicting that things would improve after Genscher resigned, I proved too optimistic. He was succeeded by Klaus Kinkel who, besides his career in politics, had also been Chairman of the Directorate of German Military Intelligence between 1979 and 1982. His record has been the subject of a book by Erich Schmidt-Eenboom [5]. The author reported that it was during Kinkel's direction of military intelligence that the Germans virtually took over the Yugoslav intelligence service and managed to replace pro-Yugoslavs with Croat officers known to favour secession.

German intellectuals needed to be persuaded that what was needed was a reassessment of Germany's record in the last World War. With this in mind, I wrote to Theo Sommer, the editor of *Die Zeit*, in 1994 and proposed that his paper should initiate such a study. Sommer airily conceded that, though he had studied modern history, Germany's role in Yugoslavia had largely escaped his notice. To remonstrations from me, he blamed me for being "obsessively pro-Serb".

It would seem that there is still a considerable gap between what is available in military archives and how much ordinary Germans know. There can be no doubt that Ribbentrop initiated the installation of the genocidal Pavelić in Zagreb. But others must have helped him in the maintenance of the Ustasha dictatorship from 1941 until the Germans lost the war. At the War Crimes Tribunal in Nuremberg there were no indictments against perpetrators of the holocaust in Yugoslavia. On this topic, many — though certainly not all — Germans still indulge in collective amnesia.

## Footnotes

1. Goebbels, Joseph (1982). *Diaries 1939-1941*. Pan Books. London.

2. Steinberg, Jonathan (1990). *All or Nothing: the Axis and the Holocaust 1941-1943*. Routledge, London / New York.

3. Wynaendts, Henry (1993). *L'engrenage. Chroniques Yougoslaves Juillet 1991 - Aôut 1992*. Editions Denoel, Paris.

4. Vernet, Daniel (1994). *Le Reve Sacrifie*. Editions Odile Jacob, Paris.

5. Schmidt-Eenboom, Erich (1995). *Der Schattenkrieger — Klaus Kinkel und der BND* [acronym for German Military Intelligence]. Econ, Dusseldorf.

Returning Bosnian Muslim POWs.

East Mostar, Bosnia and Hercegovina. 20 March 1994.

# 7

# Washington's Clout

In the summer of 1991, all 32 member-states of the Council for Security and Cooperation in Europe (CSCE) appeared committed to preserving the state of Yugoslavia. Their attitude was summarised by James Baker, who was President Bush's Secretary of State at that time. Addressing a meeting of the International Relations Committee of the US House of Representatives, on 12th January 1995, Baker declared that, in 1991, it was widely appreciated that if unilateral declarations of independence demolished Yugoslavia, and violated the Helsinki Final Act, "that would kick off the damndest civil war they had ever seen. And that's exactly what happened."

Nine months after Baker's testimony, Colin Powell, Bush's Chief of Staff, pleaded against allowing the US armed forces to be sucked into the war. He also pointed out that "the Serbs had very good reason to be worried about being in a Muslim-dominated country. It was not just paranoia." [1]

When Bill Clinton, in his presidential campaign of 1992, committed himself to treating the shrinking little country of Serbia, with a population of less than 12 million, as America's enemy number one, he was protecting his challenged self-image. Asked by a TV interviewer to comment on Bush's Yugoslav policy, Clinton commented:     "President Bush's policy towards the former

Yugoslavia mirrors his indifference to the massacre at Tiananmen Square and his coddling of Saddam Hussein. Once again the Administration is turning its back on violations of human rights and our own democratic values." From that time on, it was indispensable that Clinton should show himself less "wimpish" than President Bush.

Having become president himself, and having to prepare for his 1996 re-election campaign, Clinton had to resist his reputation as a draft dodger (he evaded military service during the Vietnam war). In Washington DC a sick joke did the rounds: "Hell hath no fury like a draft dodger who then finds himself in charge of the army, navy and air force."

It is still open to question whether or not, if Clinton had stayed neutral, the subsequent Bosnian conflict could have been averted. In March 1992 in Lisbon, before the fighting had started, Lord Carrington and his deputy ambasador Cutileiro had negotiated what was called a "cantonal" deal, which was initialled by the Bosnian Muslims, Serbs and Croats. This plan, supported by elaborate maps, provided that each district or municipality would be declared a "canton" and would be ruled by the community which was locally in the majority.

The Bosnian Serbs welcomed what they felt was the preservation of their national rights. The vice-president of the newly-elected government of the Serb Republic, Nikola Koljević, was visiting London at the time. After hearing that an agreement had been reached, he told me he thought the risks of civil war had been overcome at the eleventh hour.

Warren Zimmermann, the US ambassador in Belgrade, was less pleased and travelled to Sarajevo to encourage Izetbegović to rethink his adhesion. Zimmermann later told *The New York Times* correspondent, David Binder, that, on reflection, his initiative might have been a mistake. But the Washington stance was hardening, [2] and what seems to have started as Zimmermann's personal action was never repudiated by his chiefs.

A mistake often made by critics of US policy is to oversimplify the guidelines directing Clinton's policy. Among the President's aides, consideration of the coming election was certainly a dominant issue. And each of the aides was eager to be closer than his rivals to the President's way of thinking. This, however, was far from easy, as Clinton himself frequently shifted his own beliefs about what could and should be done.

A valuable analysis of the muddles and confusions within Clinton's team is contained in Elizabeth Drew's book, *On The Edge: The Clinton Presidency*. As Drew shows, the bizarre performances of Clinton's advisors, which so often baffled visiting Europeans, came from the President's own uncertainty. Drew likens him to "a cork bobbing in the waves." [3]

Having denounced Bush's "wimpishness", Clinton selected the hard-liner Tony Lake to be his National Security Advisor. Lake put together an aggressive package summed up in the epithet: "Lift and Strike." This meant lifting the arms embargo against the recognised Izetbegović government and delivering air strikes to compel the Serbs to accept incorporation into a Muslim-led Bosnia. In the spring of 1992, the French and British, who had troops in Bosnia, strongly objected: they feared that, in the event of air strikes, their men would become vulnerable as potential hostages.

What we learn from Drew is that, by the summer, Mr. and Ms. Clinton had read, and were personally moved by, an account of the Yugoslav collapse written by Robert D. Kaplan [4]. It was subsequently revealed that, while writing, Kaplan had treasured a copy of Rebecca West's *magnum opus*, *Black Lamb and Grey Falcon* [5], and that Kaplan shared with West an underlying sympathy for the tribulation of the Serbs.

During the period in 1992 when the Clintons had put their anti-Serb belligerence on hold, four state department officials resigned in protest against Washington's inactivity. The most articulate of these was George Kenney, who had been working on the Yugoslav desk. He later revealed that he had no background knowledge whatever of the Balkans and had never been to Yugoslavia [6].

By this time, the Croat and Muslim lobbies had whipped up emotions and sold the idea that the Serbs were guilty of genocide. Kenney later recalled that when he first addressed a meeting to demand military action against the Serbs, he spoke "extemporaneously" for two hours and the crowd of several hundred gave him a standing ovation.

It is very much to Kenney's credit that he went on being concerned about what was really happening in Bosnia. Little by little, realities ousted his earlier illusions. His revisionist views exposed him to furious denunciations when, in January 1996, he explained why he had reversed his position in the left-wing journal, *The Nation* [7].

Kenney had spent his time carefully going through all the available evidence. He had come round to the conclusion that, for political reasons of their own, the Muslims had exaggerated the scale of the fighting. They claimed the figure of fatal casualties to be a quarter of a million. Kenney's own estimate of deaths was between 25,000 and 60,000 — not enough to substantiate the charge of genocide which had been central to the anti-Serb campaign. To this day there are no internationally corroborated figures on the casualties, but the American general, Charles G.

Boyd, who had served in Yugoslavia and also ridiculed the Muslim figures, gave the estimate of between 70,000 and 100,000 deaths [8]. Kenney has been the victim of furious denunciations, but none of his critics has been able to rebut his facts or to give figures of casualties other than those from Bosnian government sources.

Kenney also came round to the view that the Bosnian Muslim president, Alija Izetbegović, had opted for war rather than peace. Kenney met Izetbegović several times and affirmed in his article in *The Nation* that "never in the course of [our] conversations did he voice doubts about the cost of the war to the Bosnian people." On this point, Kenney felt that Izetbegović had always been consistent. He agitated constantly for international military intervention to enable him to achieve his aim of governing a single, unitary state.

By January 1996, Kenney felt able to write that it would be "almost impossible to be too anti-Serb" in the pervading climate of opinion. Kenney says that he has often been asked at what point he changed his mind, but he has always insisted that there was no sudden conversion, only a cumulative process:

"As mistrustful as I was of the Serbs generally, and aware of their culpability for the war, nevertheless I began to feel sympathy for the political dilemma they faced in the former Yugoslavia. Their search for elemental justice, however criminal their tactics, should have been considered. To be evenhanded, Washington should have treated in a procedurally equal way all the factions' claims to self-determination. It goes beyond a consideration of power balances. American interests, as I understand them, flow from our philosophical support for local political legitimacy; we should not

be in the business of imposing arbitrary solutions from above"
[9].

By the summer of 1992, the Clintons had decided to reaffirm
Washington's solidarity with the ruling Muslims. Hair-raising TV
images of the shelling of Sarajevo had done the trick. The
principle which should govern US policy had been laid down
early in the Clinton presidency by the Secretary of State, Warren
Christopher. His doctrine committed the Americans to respect
and, if necessary, to defend the borders of a unitary Bosnia and
Hercegovina. The argument rested on the fact that this state had
been admitted as a member of the UN and was thus internationally recognised as a single entity. This attitude, which was ultimately to prevail, encouraged the ruling Muslims to suppose they
could rely on US support in their on-going struggle to win the
war.

During the Washington tangles, the military branch of government was split. General Colin Powell, later urged to stand as a
presidential candidate, made no secret of his opposition to any
policy involving US forces in the Balkan civil wars. He had served
in Vietnam and saw a frightening similarity. Once again US forces
would be going into a conflict without any clearly defined war
aim or any limits on the American commitment.

A very different view, however, was being taken by some other
senior US officers, particularly those serving in Germany. Many
of these were deeply troubled by the post-cold war cuts in
military spending and were anxious for an opportunity to show
the world that the US army could distinguish itself in live action
against an identifiable enemy. It was these officers who worked
out a project to send 25,000 American troops into ex-Yugoslavia.
Unlike in Vietnam, none of the soldiers were conscripts and it was
hoped that many of them would relish something more exciting

than interminable exercises in which they made themselves a nuisance in a peaceful Germany.

The mission of the 25,000 was to change dramatically, even though the nature of the mission was to stay the same. By the end of 1992, UNPROFOR was failing to bring the war to an end and there was mounting pressure, particularly from Washington, to bring the force home. The Americans then announced an unsolicited offer to provide 25,000 men to help extract the UNPROFOR contingents. Privately, many UNPROFOR officers felt they could leave more safely and with less loss of equipment if, instead of organising a fighting withdrawal aided by the American contingent, they could use their existing experience and personal links with local commanders. They could thus arrange a negotiated withdrawal. By 1995, prospects had changed but the same 25,000 men were to be sent in, this time for the purpose of imposing an American solution.

Another US general who shares Powell's dread of seeing US forces sucked into unwinnable civil wars is General Charles Boyd, mentioned above. Boyd, now retired, had done 35 years of active service and from November 1992 until July 1995 had been Deputy Commander of US Forces in Europe. He had risen to the rank of general in Vietnam and had seen the Yugoslav conflicts "up close". He described his experiences in an article for *Foreign Affairs*, in which he denounced US policy for being "based on a tragic ignorance or disregard of history" [10].

As Boyd perceptively pointed out, all three warring communities, Serb, Muslim and Croat, were pursuing precisely the same objective: none wanted to be a minority ruled by representatives of a different and potentially hostile group. In these circumstances, Boyd protested against the US resolve to participate in the Bosnian war by backing the ruling Muslims against the

Bosnian Serbs. He rejected allegations that the Bosnian Serbs were driven by aggressive ambitions for a "Greater Serbia", the argument used by Washington as an excuse for dragging the US into the war:

"The linchpin of the US approach has been the under-informed notion that this is a war of good versus evil, of aggressor against aggrieved. From that premise the US has supported UN and NATO resolutions couched in seemingly neutral terms — for example, to protect peacekeepers — and then has turned them around to punish one side and attempt to affect the course of the war."

Clinton's resolve to disregard the Powell / Boyd warning and to make war against the Bosnian Serbs might have left him liable to charges of arbitrary action. What his aides knew he needed — and what they managed to get for him — was a device to reassure US opinion formers that Washington policy was strictly in accordance with international law. It was for this purpose that the peculiar International Criminal Tribunal for the former Yugoslavia was set up at The Hague in 1993. Its mandate was at first limited to ex-Yugoslavia but was later extended to include Rwanda.

The groundwork for the Tribunal was prepared by what claimed to be an "expert commission" which was entrusted with the task of cross-questioning Muslims and Croats to obtain testimony on war crimes perpetrated by the Serbs. The man behind this task force was the American-Hungarian billionaire, George Soros. Like many Hungarians, Soros had a built-in animosity to the Serbs that went back to Hungarian objections over the creation of Yugoslavia, when Hungary had been deprived of Vojvodina.

Soros was more than willing to help Clinton demonise the Serbs. His "expert commission" was quite separate from the UN and operated not in New York but in the Catholic De Paul University in Chicago. From the atrocities alleged by the "expert commission" to the setting up of a war crimes tribunal was only one short step. The new court, installed by the UNSC at The Hague, claimed to be modelled on the Nuremberg Tribunal. But, unlike Nuremberg, the country in question was not occupied and did not have possession of the alleged villains.

The political purposes of the new court were hard to conceal. In the years between Nuremberg and the creation of The Hague Tribunal, there had been some 34 civil wars, many of them costing far more lives than the conflicts in ex-Yugoslavia. Some of these wars, notably in Cambodia and Angola, were still going on in 1993. Yet Washington has never felt it necessary to show why "justice" was required only in the case of Yugoslavia. In the summer of 1993, the court's remittance was extended to Rwanda, where deaths were numbered in tens of thousands. Though many Rwandans are in jail, no African has so far been put on trial.

Washington has insisted that the present federal state of Yugoslavia, composed of Serbia and Montenegro, be deprived of the right to continue to represent Yugoslavia. There is some dispute over the criteria by which the rights of succession are established. As noted earlier, representatives of the present Yugoslavia argue, with some justification, that they have as much right to succession as did India or Russia. Both countries, after part of their own territories had seceded, have been treated as legitimate successors.

A minor spat at the UN reveals underlying embarrassment. International jurists, mainly from the UN staff, had put together a 137-page document dealing with the wider problems of recognition and secession. Two sentences allowed the Serbs to claim that the document contained an implicit admission that the rump

Yugoslavia qualified to retain the rights of the Yugoslavia which existed before the present conflicts. It did not take long for Washington to see that, if this interpretation could be maintained, their whole case would collapse. After some secret negotiations, the two offending sentences were struck out and the text was officially endorsed without them.

It is as a leading member of the NATO alliance that the US exercises its clout. The preservation of NATO solidarity is a top priority for many West European governments, including the UK. The treaty, which provides US nuclear cover to its members, is felt to be vital as long as the ex-USSR, notably Russia, may once again impose a nuclear threat. In these circumstances not even France, NATO's most recalcitrant member state, dares challenge the policies of the President of the United States. President Clinton's personal clout became all the stronger after his re-election on 5 November 1996.

**Footnotes**

1. General Colin Powell, as reported by Henry Louis Gates, Jr. *The New Yorker*, (25 September 1995).

2. Lord Carrington accuses the Americans of rejecting this agreement, stating that "hundreds of thousands dead, millions ethnically cleansed and mass destruction, all that may not have happened if everything was left to Yugoslavs." (*NIN*, 24 October 1995). Similarly, withe the Owen-Staltenberg Plan, the journalists who lunched with Izetbegović on 1 September 1993 were confidently predicting that a deal would be signed later in the day. However, unknown to EC / UN negotiators, President Clinton's representative Charles Redman advised Izetbegović the same afternoon that US would support his additional demands and negotiations broke down (*The Independent*, September 3, 1993).

3. Drew, Elizabeth (1994). *On The Edge: The Clinton Presidency.* Simon and Shuster.

4. Kaplan, Robert D. (1993). *Balkan Ghosts.* St. Martin's Press.

5. West, Rebecca (1942). *Black Lamb and Grey Falcon.* Macmillan.

6. Kenney, George (8-15 January 1996). *The Nation.*

7. *Ibid.*

8. Boyd, General Charles G. (September / October 1995). *Foreign Affairs*, Volume 74, No. 5.

9. Kenney, George (8-15 January 1996). *The Nation.*

10. Boyd, General Charles G. (September / October 1995). *Foreign Affairs*, Volume 74, No. 5.

Milivoje Ivanišević inspecting destroyed tank.

Drina Valley. 15 April 1994.

# 8

# Pan-Islamic Ascendancy

The Muslims are now the largest religious / national community in what is currently recognised as the state of Bosnia. Given both the continued exodus of Bosnian Serbs and Bosnian Croats, and the high Muslim birthrate, it is almost certain that, at the turn of the century, the Muslims will constitute an absolute majority.

The Bosnian Muslims, like other Muslim communities scattered around the world, have split among themselves. The basic division is between the modernists, who willingly adjust to secular society, and the pan-Islamicists, who are dedicated to theocratic Muslim rule. According to the pan-Islamicists' view, Koranic law has to prevail.

Early in the current conflict it looked as if the modernisers might dominate. In the elections to the presidium in 1990, most votes went to Fikret Abdić, the former head of a large agro-industrial complex in the Bihać region northwest of Bosnia. As General Boyd has written, Fikret Abdić represented "one of the few examples of successful multi-ethnic cooperation in the Balkans." [1] For a while, Abdić managed to run his own autonomous region, working easily with Croats and Serbs. Later the pan-Islamic army, militarily and diplomatically supported by the Americans, drove him out. The region was captured and Abdić took asylum in Croatia. His story is far from over. He has already said that he and his followers will contest the next elections.

Another modernised Muslim who came near to imposing himself was the former Partisan officer, Adil Zulfikarpašić. After the last world war he emigrated to Zurich, where he made his fortune. In the summer of 1991, while fighting was going on between the Croats and Serbs, Zulfikarpašić resolved to return to Bosnia and do what he could to prevent a similar civil war between the Serbs and Muslims. In July 1991 Zulfikarpašić met the Serb leader, Radovan Karadžić, and induced him to commit himself to helping preserve the two communities from inter-tribal violence.

By this time, Alija Izetbegović had emerged as leader of the Bosnian Muslims and Zulfikarpašić assumed that Izetbegović would support such a peace deal. Though Izetbegović later presented himself to the Western world as eager to preserve Yugoslavia, the chronicle of events shows this was never so. A Serb delegation led by the well-known writer and politician, Dobrica Ćosić, visited Izetbegović in Sarajevo early in 1991. They discovered, to their horror, that he was already implacably resolved to set up a state of his own. None of this, however, was known to Zulfikarpašić, who said he had been given to understand that Izetbegović would be a cosignatory of any Muslim / Serb deal.

According to Zulfikarpašić's own account [2], Karadžić helped him organise mass rallies at which thousands of representatives from both communities committed themselves enthusiastically to living peacefully together.   There were large gatherings, notably at Trebinje and Zvornik, where there were not the faintest signs of inter-community animosities.

Zulfikarpašić tells us that everyone knew which towns or villages were primarily Serb and which were Muslim. Under the peace plan, the majority communities would head the administration but also be responsible for defending the minority. While Zulfikarpašić was negotiating, however, Izetbegović visited America for a few weeks. On his return, he dramatically demolished Zulfikarpašić's initiative. From July 1991, Izetbegović and the SDA ran a hostile campaign, treating Zulfikarpašić as a traitor to the Muslim cause. Soon afterwards he went back to Switzerland, where he still resides.

The rise and dominance of Izetbegović's new party, the SDA, marked the end of any hope of a peaceful reconciliation between the three communities. Some critics of the SDA have tried to portray Izetbegović himself as a religious fanatic. He is nothing of the sort: he knows no Arabic, has never studied the Koran and has learnt what he needs to know about Islam only through reading extracts translated into Serbo-Croat or English.

What really distinguished Izetbegović from many of his co-religionaries was not religious learning but his commitment to the pan-Islamic cause. He defended the concept of a single, theocratic, pan-Islamic entity stretching from Morocco to Indonesia. In all the areas where Islam prevailed, the laws of the Koran would be introduced.

It was his anti-secular commitment that induced Izetbegović to be one of the early members of the "Mladi Musilmani" [Young Muslims] movement, created in 1941 when he was only 16 years old. As could have been anticipated, immediately after the Second World War Izetbegović's movement came into conflict with Titoist communists. In 1946 he and his group were arrested and he served three years in jail. He was to serve another term between 1983 and 1988, also for separatist agitation.

Izetbegović set forth his opinions in *The Islamic Declaration* [3], which was so extreme that many observers wondered whether it was indeed his own work or a forgery intended to disgrace him. The text was highly Manichean, with all spirituality, goodness and dynamism coming from the Islamic side and all the corruption, consumerism and self-indulgence identified with the West. The principal enemies, however, were the Muslims who had allowed themselves to be assimilated and were living comfortably within a secular society.

It was only after consulting the Arabist specialists in the British Foreign Office that I learnt that the text, far from being marginal, was well in line with exactly the same kind of screeds being widely circulated within pan-Islamic circles.

While Izetbegović was in jail in the 1980s, his supporters in the USA published a book for which he also claimed authorship: *Islam between East and West*. Like *The Declaration*, the text proclaimed the superiority of Islam over any other religion and insisted on the duty of the Muslims to install theocratic government in any areas where they were in the majority.

In a TV documentary spelling out the new party's aspirations for a revival of Muslim ascendancy, Izetbegović, backed by his old friends from the Young Muslims, took the leading role [4]. In his version of history, the Muslims (in this context he did not distinguish between the Turks and the Slavs) had come to grief on three separate occasions. He noted that each of the bad years ended with the figure eight.

The first came in 1878, when Austro-Hungary occupied Bosnia and Hercegovina and drove out many of the Turkish educated elite. The second misfortune came in 1908, when Austro-Hungary unilaterally annexed the province, which led to another exodus of Turks. The third was 1918: when Yugoslavia was formed there was another flight of Muslims to Turkey. Nonetheless, Izetbegović was able to reassure his cheering companions that all was not lost. From then on, he said, he and the SDA would revive the struggle for Muslim ascendancy.

The aim was more easily proclaimed than achieved. In reality the ruling party found itself in a cleft stick. If they wanted, as they did, to achieve a unitary Bosnia under their own control, they would be militarily incapable of implementing their goals without active support from American leaders. In the post-communist era, the Americans and the Germans played the central role and Western support could not be obtained without endorsing Western concepts of a tolerant, multi-ethnic society. On the other hand, this was at variance with Izetbegović's public record and it collided with the message which he and his ministers were constantly carrying to the East. There, the SDA depended primarily on Iran, Saudi Arabia and Iraq.

The SDA managed to preserve credibility both in the West and East. Any exposure of Izetbegović's special relations with Teheran would not have suited Clinton's anti-Serb policy. Washington systematically suppressed any item of news which would weaken Clinton's commitment to punishing the Serbs.

In some cases it was impossible to conceal the contradictions. Some liberals pleaded in vain with Izetbegović to repudiate the *fatwa* against Salman Rushdie. Rushdie, himself blissfully ignorant of the realities in Sarajevo (which he had never visited), took it into his own head to declare his total emotional dedication to the cause of the Bosnian Muslims. Within three days of an article by Rushdie in *The Guardian* [5], a member of Izetbegović's government denounced him as a traitor. In an article translated into English and published in the London based *Muslim News* [6], the Bosnian Minister for special production (a euphemism for military output) denounced Rushdie and his friends as the incarnation of evil:

"Through careful reading of even this small Rushdie essay about Sarajevo, it is possible to conclude that he is one of the advocates of Satanic forces that turn to dust and ashes all they can in this country. He speaks the same words so often spoken by Milošević, Karadžić, Tuđman, Boban ..."

Izetbegović's pre-eminence did not stay unchallenged. His old friend and ally Haris Silajdžić, who had been such a central figure of the SDA governments, emerged by the mid-1990s as his most formidable rival. Silajdžić is endowed with extraordinary diplomatic talents and has managed better than Izetbegović to persuade his Western public that he favours a tolerant, secular state. Yet he travels persistently and delivers precisely the opposite message to the fundamentalist states in the Middle East. UN officers on the ground believe that he became rich through black market dealings. It was Silajdžić, while still in the Izetbegović government, who successfully agitated for the withdrawal of UN forces in favour of the more anti-Serb, US-led NATO.

From the 1970s, Silajdžić had been well known in academic circles as a leading anti-modernizer. He had completed his studies in Libya and it was not until the 1990s that he switched from academic to political activity. His exceptional gifts ensured him a central role, and on 2 October 1994 the Slovene newspaper *Delo* first revealed that he was no longer a collaborator with Izetbegović, but a rival.

Silajdžić's double-talk was made easier by his blatant disregard of factual evidence. On 15th January 1995 he told a televised news conference, attended by General Sir Michael Rose, that Rose was personally responsible for the deaths of 70,000 civilians in the Bihać region. As UN officers later confirmed, the total casualties around Bihać had been around 1,000 — mostly fighting men.

At the beginning of 1996, Silajdžić resigned from the Izetbegović government and formed a party of his own. At the time of writing this book it is too soon to say which of the rival Muslim groups will prevail. For the time being NATO has managed to impose a temporary truce but it seems likely that, after the US pull-out, there will be a further descent into chaos and anarchy. The prospects suggest another Afghanistan, where, in a vicious civil war which has lasted until now, the Americans armed all the Muslim groups and let them fight it out with each other.

## Footnotes

1. Boyd, General Charles G. (September / October 1995). *Foreign Affairs*, Volume 74 No. 5.

2. Adil Zulfikarpašić's conversations with Milovan Djilas and Nadezda Gace, *Bosnjacki Institut*, Zurich, 1994.

3. Izetbegović, Alija (republished 1990). *The Islamic Declaration*. Sarajevo.

4. TV documentary (1990). *Muslimani — od imena do kongresa* [*Muslims — From the Name to the Congress*]. Sarajevo.

5. Rushdie, Salman (25 April 1994). *Index on Censorship* 1/2. (reprinted in *The Guardian*).

6. Čehajić, Rusmir Mahmud (27th April 1994). *Muslim News*.

7. *Panorama*, BBC Television, 23 January 1995.

Press briefing by Bosnian Serb Officer and UNPROFOR Commander.

Brčko, Republika Srpska. 11 May 1994.

# 9

# The Unbalanced
# Western Media

"The reporting and commenting of some members of the press corps in Sarajevo became close to becoming identified to the propaganda machine of the Bosnian government." The former British commander in Sarajevo, General Sir Michael Rose, delivered this verdict in a lecture at All Souls College, Oxford, on 23 February 1996. It exposed the very real frustrations and indignation of Western peacekeepers who were constantly being bludgeoned and denounced by Western journalists and TV image makers.

In analysing the role of the Western media a distinction has to be made between writing journalists and TV performers. The journalists were, for the most part, pontificators who had previously pronounced themselves on many other world issues. They felt they were addressing not only their readers but also policymakers, on whom they lavished advice. Few of them — and none of the most prominent — had intimate background knowledge of how the present problems started. The fighting, as we have seen, began not because of a Serb or Belgrade craving for a "Greater Serbia", but because of the much more localised rage of peasant farmers living in the contested territory. The overwhelming majority of Serb communities, in what the international community recognised as Croatia and Bosnia, rebelled, and were ready to use force to prevent themselves being integrated into what seemed to them alien and hostile statelets.

On the side of the journalists, two stood out: Misha Glenny, who had been the BBC correspondent in Vienna, and Michael Ignatieff, who made his reputation as an expert on Russia. Their influence extended to both sides of the Atlantic. *The New York Review of Books*, which sets the tone for most articulate American intellectuals, opened its columns only to these two or those who held the same views. The editor of the *Review*, Robert Silvers, flatly rejected suggestions that the paper had an obligation to take a longer term view and ought to commission articles examining how the conflict really started.

Glenny published his book, *The Fall of Yugoslavia* [1], in the summer of 1992, just as the war was spreading to Bosnia. The book was highly readable and was read by most of the members of the Western media sent to Sarajevo. But Glenny's book focussed on his own eye-witness accounts, and failed to dig out the evidence on the origins of the conflict.

Glenny, knowing nothing about the local Serb communities, blamed what he rightly saw as a detestable war exclusively on Belgrade and, more specifically, on the Serb leader, Slobodan Milošević, whom Glenny charged with the aim of creating a "Greater Serbia". As we have seen, this was an illusion: Milošević was pondering how to retain power and he was under considerable popular pressure to help the Serb communities outside Serbia. Having incriminated Serbia, Glenny called for international military intervention against "Greater Serbia".

In handling the record of the Croat leader, Franjo Tuđman, and his Ustasha supporters, Glenny was far more indulgent. Yet it was this racialist partnership which was the prime reason for  the bust-up of Yugoslavia and the consequent conflict. Glenny went no further than criticising what he called the "ham-fistedness" of the Croat leadership in failing to make sufficient allowances for what, in Glenny's mind, was "the almost psychotic sensitivity" of the Serb peoples. He would not have used the word "psychotic" had he been more familiar with events in World War Two.

Though Glenny went some way towards exculpating Tuđman, the innocent martyrs of Glenny's account are the Bosnian Muslims. In later years Glenny produced several updated versions of his influential book. But, though he became a little less cocksure about just what the Western world should do, he never deviated from advocating support for the Bosnian Muslim leaders.

It was the same unwillingness to examine the origins of the conflict that flawed the second pontificator, Michael Ignatieff. In the early months of the war (September 1992), Ignatieff wrote to me: "I know enough about the Yugoslav situation to realise that blame for the catastrophe should be apportioned among all parties." In subsequent years, such neutrality vanished.

Ignatieff fully endorsed the Croat version of what happened in Vukovar. A very different account came from the direct testimony of Dr. Zoran Stanković, a forensic scientist with an international reputation for rectitude. Dr. Stanković had been present when the Yugoslav army went into Vukovar. Dr. Stanković says that he saw some 700 bodies which the Croats had left lying in the roads.

By this time, however, Ignatieff's mind was closed. Rather than engage in research on the ground, it was a lot easier for him to hitch a ride round several of the African states with Boutros Boutros-Ghali and senior members of the UN. In going with them, he accepted their delusion that all inter-ethnic and inter-tribal conflicts were much of a muchness. In an article for *The*

*New Yorker,* [2] Ignatieff described the trip and endorsed the misleading UN view that you could learn about Bosnia by witnessing troubles in Angola.

As the years drew on, Ignatieff was increasingly sucked into that group which had been identified by General Rose as spokesmen for the Muslim propaganda machine. Reviewing David Owen's book, *Balkan Odyssey,* [3] in *The New York Review of Books* [4], Ignatieff declared: "It is difficult to think of a recent conflict where there was such a moral unanimity and so little determination to do anything about it."

Ignatieff fully supported Owen's own view that, if only sufficient force had been used against the Bosnian Serbs, they could have been bombed or shelled into submission two years sooner. Owen and Ignatieff claimed that when the Croats and Muslims launched their offensive in 1995, they were "re-conquering land taken from them in 1992." [5] This illustrates their basic misunderstanding. As we have seen, most of the land under dispute was owned by Serb peasants who felt that they were fighting to protect their farms and families.

Shutting his eyes to this uncomfortable reality, Ignatieff joined Owen in developing a personal loathing of the Bosnian Serbs: "It would be grotesque to forget that the siege of Sarajevo was initiated and maintained by the Serbs." [6] — He should have placed this action within the context of Serb resistance to forcible incorporation into a Muslim state. He added: "Most of the war crimes in Bosnia, including the murder of many thousands of civilians and military personnel, were committed by Serbs." [7]

Ignatieff does not tell us the sources of these latest atrocity stories, but they could only have come from the Muslim propaganda machine. Ignatieff went even further, claiming that the Serb Republic — now internationally recognised as a separate entity — was "a creation of war criminals." [8] He forgot, though he must at one time have known, that the Bosnian Serb Republic had been set up as a result of the declared will of most Bosnian Serbs. The 1990 elections, provided the Bosnian Serbs with 88 seats in the Bosnia assembly. 86 of these went to Radovan Karadžić and his nationalist party. The same elections gave legitimacy to Izetbegović's SDA party.

Few of the internationally-recognised pundits have stopped to examine just why Karadžić has consistently pleaded for a division of Bosnia into its three national / religious components. This has been interpreted simply as the intolerance and xenophobia of the Bosnian Serbs. What should be remembered, however, is that Karadžić was leading a community that refused to become part of a Muslim-led Bosnia and had been struggling for years to assert its own identity. In Karadžić's view, which did not change after 1991, all three peoples would feel safe only when ruled by members of the same group. Peaceful coexistence had at first seemed possible both to Karadžić and Zulfikarpašić. In practice, when Izetbegović reasserted the Bosnian Muslims' claim to ascendancy, Karadžić retaliated by demanding the separation of the three groups. Events have strengthened his insistence that the three peoples could not, at least for the foreseeable future, coexist within the same slabs of land.

Unlike the print journalists, the TV image-makers had quicker access to fame and also a more immediate and dramatic ability to influence policy-making. There has been some argument on the question of how far what came out of "the box" effectively controlled what policies were subsequently adopted. What is certain is that many televised horror stories, originating with Muslim propaganda, created a mood in which democratically elected politicians on either side of the Atlantic felt they "had to do something." Screams of outrage following a particularly lurid

TV image required at least some semblance of action. Several Western politicians, including the former British Foreign Secretary, Douglas Hurd, have publicly admitted that TV images themselves ruled out non-intervention.

The TV image makers required talents different from those of writing journalists. Besides physical courage (some lost their lives in Muslim / Serb crossfire during the fighting within the Sarajevo region), the image makers also needed to be what the French would call *debrouillard* (a capability for solving complex practical problems). What the TV reporters and cameramen needed above all was the ability to cope with the exigences of their home-based editors and bosses. What these demanded were brief, simple soundbites, available on time and providing material sufficiently hair-raising or tear-jerking to qualify for inclusion in TV news bulletins or documentaries.

The editors agreed that coverage should be from Sarajevo, which gave the Muslim government an enormous advantage. What the TV operators needed to be able to provide at any moment was easily available material. There was neither inclination nor time to examine whether the soundbites so conveyed represented reality, or were a product of the local propaganda machine.

From the need for the story to be simple, with goodies and baddies clearly distinguished, it was only one stop to suppressing any stories suggesting that the Serbs themselves were, in many cases, the victims. There were several cases in which images of Serb victims were rearranged to suggest to viewers that the corpses were Muslim. Several correspondents later reported that they got to know that it was a waste of time and effort trying to file images of Serb suffering as these would only alienate home-based directors. The CNN took the lead in delivering appropriate

soundbites, sparing viewers from any complicated moral dilemma: the Muslims were good, the Serbs bad.

A book published in 1995 by Martin Bell [9], the British TV star,
gives us useful clues about the way in which the TV herd clung
together in friendly proximity. The book also reveals the impact
which sudden celebrity had on the personality of the performer.
Bell revealed that he considered himself "morally superior" to
the British officers on the ground. While the officers were seen as
"appeasers" (i.e. willing to negotiate with the Bosnian Serbs),
Bell identified himself with the Muslim cause.

Refusing to conceive of the Bosnian Muslims as anything but
innocent victims, Bell, arriving in Sarajevo in April 1992, summarily denied Serb claims that the Muslims had initiated the killing
and the Serbs had retaliated. In reality, the Muslims, who had
been in the majority along part of the Drina valley, took advantage of their superiority to eliminate whole villages of Serbs.
When the Bosnian Serbs re-grouped their forces and were able
to dominate the disputed territory, they collected ample docu-
mentation on what happened. The man most responsible for the
dossiers was Milivoje Ivanišević [10], a Serb academic who relied
for his evidence on autopsies carried out on the Serb corpses
found along the Drina valley. The villagers knew each other and,
through elaborate interrogation, were able to identify not only
the names of those killed but often the names of many of the
killers.

In rejecting such embarrassing evidence, Bell had placed himself
at the disposal of the man who became his mentor, Haris Silajdžić.
As we have seen, Silajdžić was a cunning operator, and Bell
seemed to fall under his spell. This meant that, in selecting news

items, little could be included which might have seemed favourable to the Bosnian Serbs.

A great deal of hard evidence has accumulated showing that, on several occasions, the Bosnian government arranged to kill their own people exclusively for the sake of incriminating the Serbs. Bell would have known of this through his close contacts with British UN officers, but he ignored what they might have told him. In order to fall into line with Silajdžić, the allegations were dismissed as impossible or unthinkable.

Bell did not want to appear personally anti-Serb, so he responded, as Silajdžić did, by lauding the small number of Bosnian Serbs who stayed in the Muslim sector of Sarajevo and who were willing to work with the Bosnian government. What Bell failed to reveal was that these Serbs represented only a small proportion of the Bosnian Serb community.

To help the Bosnian Muslims do everything possible to incriminate the Bosnian Serbs, the bias of the media was further promoted by the resolve of the Clinton Administration — notably Clinton's chief advisor, Tony Lake. This led to subterfuges which contradicted the generally accepted principles of accountable government. According to David Owen's account [11], which has never been challenged, Western experts discovered that it was the Bosnian Muslims, not the Bosnian Serbs, who had fired the grenade in February 1994 which fell on the Markale market place. This was alleged to have killed 68 people, and led to calls for punitive air strikes against the Bosnian Serbs. According to Owen, at a moment when UNPROFOR wanted the Bosnian Muslims to participate in truce negotiations, the British commander, General Rose, blackmailed the Bosnian Muslim leaders into submission. He told them that unless they agreed to cooperate, he would tell the international press that he had technical expertise proving that the grenade came from the Muslim, not the Serb, side.

Because the Bosnian leadership acquiesced, the distortion was never exposed. Owen felt that it was quite acceptable to distort the evidence if this helped to promote the cause of the Bosnian government and cause further damage to Izetbegović's enemies, the Bosnian Serbs. The deliberate misinformation of the general public seems not to have troubled him.

In retrospect, the degree of credulity with which Western opinion accepted Muslim propaganda may seem astonishing. It might have seemed likelier that Western opinion would side with the Christians (i.e. the Serbs and Croats) rather than the Muslims, whose special relations with Teheran were widely known.

It was the TV images which decided otherwise. The power these exercised on adult populations evokes a story from *The Winter's Tale*: a peasant girl goes off to hear Autolycus's wild fabrications and returns to tell a crowd: "I saw it writ down, and so I know 'tis true." The modern equivalent is the TV viewer who, having seen pictures with his or her own eyes, is quite sure these must represent what is really happening in Bosnia.

## Footnotes

1. Glenny, Misha *(1992). The Fall of Yugoslavia.* Penguin.

2. Ignatieff, Michael (14 August 1995). *The New Yorker.*

3. Owen, David (1995). *Balkan Odyssey.* Gollancz.

4. Ignatieff, Michael (29 February 1996). *New York Review of Books.*

5. *Ibid.*

6. *Ibid.*

7. *Ibid.*

8. *Ibid.*

9. Bell, Martin *(1995). In Harm's Way — Reflections of a War Zone Thug.* Hamish Hamilton.

10. Ivanišević, Milivoje *(1994). Hronika Našeg Groblja — ili slovo o stradanju srpskog naroda Bratunca, Milića, Skelana i Srebrnice* [*The Chronicle of our Graveyards — description of the suffering of the Serbian people of Bratunac, Milići, Skelani and Srebrenica*]. Belgrade.

11. Owen, David (1995). *Balkan Odyssey.* Gollancz.

French UNPROFOR soldier on guard duty.
Bridge of Brotherhood and Unity, Sarajevo. 14 May 1994.

# 10

# Disaster at Dayton

As the 1996 presidential elections approached, Tony Lake's pressure for military intervention in Bosnia became increasingly effective. And once he had won the day, he was able to give his friend, the formidable operator, Richard Holbrooke, the task of imposing an American solution on all the problems of ex-Yugoslavia. In doing so, Holbrooke would justify Clinton's claim to be the leader of the world.

Holbrooke knew singularly little about the peoples who lived in ex-Yugoslavia, even though he had long been a prominent veteran on international affairs. In 1992 he had made a couple of brief trips to the region and from what he said — which was very little — he had made up his mind that the Serbs were the guilty party. The Americans, he felt, could easily bring them to heel. Since then, he had constantly agitated to be allowed to handle the job himself. His thinking was much influenced by the then American ambassador in Sarajevo, who told a British officer that he regarded his mission as one of gaining support for the Izetbegović government.

Holbrooke's earlier international experience went back to the Vietnam war. His first diplomatic posting was in Saigon and the then president, Jimmy Carter, had promoted him to be Assistant Secretary of State for Asian and East Pacific Affairs. During the

Reagan and Bush era, having identified with the Democrats, Holbrooke pulled out of Washington and made his fortune on Wall Street. His driving personality and his gambling instincts stood him in good stead.

Once the Democrats returned to office, he was all set for promotion. In 1992 he became Clinton's ambassador to Germany and it was from the German perspective that he watched the war developing in ex-Yugoslavia. In 1993 he was again promoted to Assistant Secretary of State, but this time not of Asian but of European and Canadian affairs.

There were, as we have seen, outspoken divisions among Clinton's aides. Holbrooke, though nominally Assistant Secretary, was infuriated by his impotence in implementing his anti-Serb policies. Even though he was a member of the Administration, he let everyone know how much he despised Washington's irresolution.

His personal ignorance of conditions on the ground in ex-Yugoslavia shocked and astounded senior UNPROFOR officers who, after his appointment in 1994, were called in to brief him. At the start of a two-hour meeting, Holbrooke was under the illusion that Bosnia was primarily a Muslim state (in fact the Christians were a majority) and was being invaded by Serb aggressors. But he was too clever to be impervious to evidence and learnt, then and there, that the Serbs engaged in the fighting were Bosnians themselves and felt that they were defending their homes and farms. From then on Holbrooke endorsed, as a precondition of a deal, the right of the Bosnian Serbs to preserve their own Serb republic. Nonetheless, Holbrooke remained as adamant as ever that, given a free hand, he could subdue the Serbs.

Confident of his capacity to impose an American plan, Holbrooke sent off repeated memoranda and letters to top people. His failure to elicit any effective replies led him, by early 1995, to think seriously of retirement. It was only after the Serb capture of the enclaves of Srebrenica and Žepa that Washington's position hardened, and, on 4th August 1995, Holbrooke realised his ambition. He was appointed by Lake as head of a six-man task-force, with full freedom to work out and impose his own solutions. (Shortly afterwards, three of his team were killed in a motor accident as they drove down Mount Igman. The loss never stopped him from indefatigably soldiering on).

At the time of taking over, Holbrooke had the advantage of finding the Bosnian Serbs very much weakened. The rearmament of the Croats, Bosnian Croats and Muslims, sanctioned by Washington, had shifted the balance of fire-power. The US-led bombing campaign of September / October 1995 weakened the Bosnian Serbs badly and destroyed Mladić's air defence and communications system. He thus lost his ability to command and control the Bosnian Serb army.

By the time Mladić saw Holbrooke, he was desperate to end the fighting. Milošević could not ignore the risks to Serbia proper if the Bosnian Serbs were decisively defeated. After such a defeat, Serbia would be confronted with a further batch of refugees for which it could not provide. As a consequence, the Bosnian Serbs found themselves at the mercy of Slobodan Milošević, who had an agenda very different from their own. Like Holbrooke, Milošević craved the maximising of his own role in world affairs. He was manifestly a man with whom Holbrooke could do business.

As the enmity between Milošević and Radovan Karadžić was well established, a compromise put Milošević in charge of any future negotiations. Milošević promised to take account of Bosnian Serb interests and a commitment to this effect was signed in the presence of Patriarch Pavle, head of the Orthodox Church. Milošević vowed to include Bosnian Serbs in any peace dealings and undertook to do nothing without their approval. When, in practice, he bullied and forced the Bosnian Serbs to submit to the American will, there was nothing more that the Church could do other than protest and the Patriarch withdrew his support of the projected deal.

For Holbrooke, as for David Owen before him, Milošević was affable, but he was in no position to force the Bosnian Serb leaders to do what Holbrooke wanted: an end to the siege of Sarajevo (i.e. the suspension of the Serb shelling of the Muslim part of Sarajevo and the opening of Sarajevo airport). Such measures could be negotiated only with the effective leaders of the Bosnian Serbs, and it was this imperative which provided the first of many occasions when Holbrooke had to conceal what he was really doing.

For the record, the US Administration could have nothing to do with Karadžić and Ratko Mladić, both indicted by The Hague war crimes tribunal. Yet these were the only men able to negotiate the terms which Holbrooke required. And so, on 13 September 1995, with prior approval from Tony Lake, Holbrooke went to Belgrade, ostensibly to talk to Milošević but surreptitiously to negotiate a truce with the two indicted Bosnian Serb leaders. Holbrooke's version of events, which he brashly gave to his friend Michael Kelly, was reported in *The New Yorker* [1]. According to Holbrooke, he and his military advisors spent eight hours in talks and, at three in the morning, an acceptable agreement was reached.

Only double-talk could preserve America's moralistic posture. Holbrooke wrote most of the signed document himself but he had to pretend that it came from Belgrade: "I would not put my signature to it, although my fingerprints were literally on it..." [2]

Having subdued the Serbs, Holbrooke had more trouble than he expected in dealing with the Muslim leaders. Here he was vulnerable; they never let him forget that Washington was committed to supporting the "territorial integrity" of the state which they claimed they represented. Holbrooke used two techniques in overcoming their resistance: first pleading and beseeching and, where necessary, promising concessions, regardless of whether or not they were feasible. Where this failed, he scolded and yelled until the Muslim leaders gave in. Kelly reported a particularly raucous slanging match between Holbrooke and the US-born Muslim Foreign Minister, Muhamed Sacirbey. This almost ended in blows, yet the following day the two men were again the best of friends [3].

At the time Holbrooke needed a truce it was the Bosnian Muslims , Bosnian Croats and the army of Croatia who were mounting an offensive. According to Alija Izetbegović [4], in October 1995 the Americans issued an "ultimatum" forcing the advancing armies to suspend their projected attack on the Serb city of Banja Luka. Holbrooke's account to Kelly is somewhat different. He recalled visiting Sarajevo accompanied by Brigadier General Donald L. Kerrick, whom he introduced as "the finest military-intelligence officer in the United States government." [5] He then left it to the general to warn Sarajevo that the Americans had direct evidence that the Serbs of Serbia were mobilising their army to protect the Bosnian Serbs. Whether or not this secret intelligence — nowhere else confirmed — was true, it sufficed to halt hostilities.

Once the truce was in place and NATO forces were ready to intervene to sustain it, Holbrooke felt the time had come to have his plan officially endorsed. The site which he selected for an international conference was the Wright-Patterson Air Force Base at Dayton, Ohio, and the meeting, requiring more work than he had supposed, lasted from 1 to 21 November.

To ensure maximum publicity, Holbrooke invited not only delegations from the warring groups but also representatives of governments and agencies involved in trying to settle the problems in ex-Yugoslavia. Nonetheless, he was adamant in keeping the conduct of negotiations to himself, excluding any outsiders from the talks and working day and night until he finally produced unanimous agreement. The French protested in vain that their exclusion from all meaningful discussions amounted to an insult.

What finally came out of Dayton was a vast assortment of deals and maps — almost all of which had been agreed in previous discussions. The document (without maps) was made available in Washington and covered some 200 pages. It was thanks to Holbrooke's unique capacity as a showman that he managed to present this hodgepodge as a great turning-point, moving Yugoslavia from war to peace. In reality, the truce had been agreed before Dayton; the IFOR implementation force was at the ready and, both before and after Dayton, violence continued. It was now, however, at a lower intensity and only sporadic.

Kelly, commenting on the Dayton deal in the *New Yorker* , said that Holbrooke "led the United States into a tangle of accords and commitments whose ramifications, both practical and moral, no one — including the man who made them — fully understands." [6] Unfortunately, it was not only a matter of comprehension,  although this 200-page document contained so many illogicalities that nobody could make sense of them — and very few tried.

As the Americans had already promised the Izetbegović government that they would defend the "territorial integrity" of Bosnia and Hercegovina, and hand over the whole of the province to Izetbegović's control, the Bosnian Muslim delegation refused to be in the same room as representatives of the Bosnian Serbs. These, they insisted, were war criminals. Holbrooke got round this by arranging what were called "proximity talks", in which he indefatigably shuttled between the delegations. His success rested in his willingness to use both threats of brute force and offers of concessions.

The Dayton texts, as published, constituted a double double-cross. First, it offered two propositions on Bosnia which were totally incompatible with each other. The Muslims were promised that the US would defend the "territorial integrity" of a unitary Bosnian state, while the Bosnian Serbs were led to believe they could preserve a separate Serb republic. As a typical Holbrooke device, the texts excluded the English word "republic", which might signify the recognition of a separate state. Instead, it referred only to the "Republika Srpska", implying this was a funny sounding place and not a real country at all. Instead of statehood, the Bosnian Serbs had to accept being no more than "an Entity" — a newly invented piece of diplomatic jargon designed to fill the gap between incorporation into Izetbegović's Bosnia and separate statehood.

The second double-cross contained in the Dayton texts was the assumption that a union of Croats and Muslims would represent the other "Entity". Such a union had been set up in Washington, at the beginning of 1994, to induce the Croats and Muslims to stop fighting each other and, instead, to join forces against the Serbs.

Holbrooke knew very well that this union had already turned out to be unworkable, as neither side had the least trust in the other. The mutual antagonism was both openly expressed and acted upon before, during and after Dayton. On 18 April 1996, Ivan Bender, chairman of the Croat deputies' club, declared: "There can be no question of a unified federal army." [7]

As Croat support was very important to Washington, Holbrooke found that he had to support two incompatible pledges. On the one side, the Izetbegović government was assured that the Americans would defend the territorial integrity of a single Bosnia and Hercegovina. At the same time, Holbrooke had to resign himself to the fact that a substantial slab of Hercegovina had, for the past three years, been politically and economically annexed by Croatia. That area now sends representatives to the Croat parliament.

The texts, as published, start with a two-page summary of the "General Framework Agreement", in which all the contradictions are already blatantly apparent. The third paragraph announces that all participants "welcome and endorse" arrangements recognising "the boundary demarcation between the two Entities." This was never welcomed or endorsed by the Bosnian Muslims. The next paragraph, concentrating on elections, treats the whole of Bosnia and Hercegovina as a unitary state under a single sovereign parliament. This was anathema to the Bosnian Serbs and Bosnian Croats.

The rest of the voluminous report consists of 12 annexes which need to be looked at separately. The first deals with the military matters due to be enforced by the NATO implementation force, IFOR. The annex demands that the parties respect "clear and distinct lines of demarcation" between "the Entities". In reality, despite Holbrooke's shuttling at Dayton (or perhaps because of it?), no such clear or distinct lines had ever existed. The maps, drawn and redrawn, were neither clear or distinct. In some cases, as it later emerged, busy negotiators used a felt-tipped pen: one border line could thus be drawn right through several buildings.

What the military annex failed to indicate, even though Holbrooke knew it at the time, was that the Americans had deliberately fostered Iranian aid to the Bosnian Muslims. In an interview on British TV on 4 May 1996, Holbrooke said that the Americans had been forced to turn a blind eye to the arms embargo. If they had not done so, the Bosnian Muslim government would have collapsed.

A second annex purports to deal with "Inter-Entity" boundaries but fails to mention Eastern Slavonia, the most explosive of all the issues. Even though, according to the present front lines, Eastern Slavonia is part of Croatia and not of Bosnia, there is the same threat to peace in both regions.

Another disputed region, Brčko, is mentioned but left unresolved. The city of Brčko itself is currently held by the Bosnian Serbs, who regard the whole region as strategically vital. But all three communities still live in the Brčko region as a whole and all claim that the Brčko territory belongs to them. The annex provides for the setting up of international arbitration to be presided over by a nominee of the Court of International Justice at The Hague (not to be confused with the newly formed war crimes tribunal in the same city). One paragraph of the annex lays it down that if no agreement can be reached, "things will stay the same as they are." Yet another clause declares that the arbitration will be "final and binding."

The third annex, perhaps the least realistic, lays down provisions for general elections. These are supposed to take place within six months and to be held under the supervision of the Organisation for Security and Cooperation. Holbrooke has managed to involve as many interested agencies as possible, hoping no doubt that officials from each will develop a vested interest in keeping his show on the road. Voters are ordered to register in the places where they had lived at the time of the last census in 1991: that is before the present conflicts began and before hundreds of thousands, perhaps millions, had either emigrated abroad or else left for other parts of Bosnia. Such provisions would have made sense if the previously warring groups were now reconciled to living peacefully together. In reality, the freedom of movement endorsed at Dayton exists only in theory. Within all three communities, the authorities in charge are able to decide who moves where.

The fourth annex gives Bosnia and Hercegovina a written constitution. As there were — and still are — no signs of a willingness to share power, which such a constitution would require, Holbrooke simply proclaims that the signatories "shall", "will" and "must" behave tolerantly to each other. Such rhetoric cannot conceal the fact that every day before, during and after Dayton, the communities have been doing the reverse.

Holbrooke has entitled his fifth annex "Agreement on Human Rights". But on this subject, needless to say, the definitions of the three leaderships sharply diverge. It is these divergencies which have enabled the Bosnian Muslims and Bosnian Serbs to accuse each other of repression amounting to genocide, and have also prevented the projected Croat / Muslim coalition from materialising.

Annex seven deals with the very real problem of refugees and displaced persons, which still constitutes a heavy burden on the Western conscience. In practice, however, far from easing this burden, Holbrooke's deal has accelerated the exodus and pushed tens of thousands more from their homes. In the final sessions at

Dayton, in order to secure the Bosnian Muslims' signature, Holbrooke agreed to hand over to the Izetbegović government control over a unified Sarajevo. In practice, that meant imposing Muslim rule over suburbs held by Bosnian Serbs. As senior UN officers rightly predicted, the local Serbs, rather than submit, would leave "with a suitcase or in a coffin". A renewed exodus was an embarrassment to Washington. The Americans claimed that the Bosnian Serb leaders had forced the Sarajevan Serbs to leave. This, however, is contradicted by the declarations made at the time by Karadžić and others.

In the weeks immediately following Dayton, Karadžić argued that it would be best if the Serbs still living in Sarajevo stayed in their present homes. Many of them were refugees many times over and at least 60,000 did stay where they were. But not for long: the refugees who had already experienced life under Muslim rule refused to expose themselves to further subjection. And once it became clear that most of the Serb residents were resolved to leave, the authorities in Pale did their best to facilitate transport and resettlement. These events took place in the midwinter of 1995-96. To cope with refugees and DPs, Holbrooke endorsed yet another commission, this one to be chaired by a nominee of the European Court of Human Rights. However, in countering the will of the local people, outsiders were helpless.

Another commission is set up in the eighth annex, this one mandated "to preserve" ancient monuments. Preservation might seem an inappropriate function, given the need for the identification and, if possible, salvage of the many monuments demolished in the various areas occupied by Serbs, Croats and Muslims. Holbrooke this time wheeled on the traditionally overstaffed

UNESCO, eager to find justification for its existence and so always in search of new tasks.

The ninth annex introduces a more down to earth agency, The European Bank for Reconstruction and Development, which is placed in charge of overseeing the restoration of the public utilities of Bosnia. What the annex fails to divulge is how much of the damage to public utilities is the direct consequence of the civil war. The American general, Charles Boyd, pinpointed the way in which shortages provided useful propaganda material [8]. He recalled that, during the winter of 1993-94, UNPROFOR specialists discovered outlets and techniques which would have enabled them to put fresh water into Sarajevo pipes. The rescue operation was prohibited by the Muslim government, nominally on the grounds of health. But, as Boyd and his fellow officers knew, the Muslim government was unwilling to forfeit poignant TV images of sad Sarajevans queuing for water. Such pictures were particularly precious when the queues lined up in areas where Muslims and Serbs were sniping at each other.

The eleventh and last annex hands back to the UN the responsibility for policing the Dayton accords. Carl Bildt, a Swedish politician who was known to favour a unitary Bosnian state, was selected to head the civilian team. From the moment of his appointment, he protested that all the money and resources were being lapped up by IFOR's military needs and hardly anything was left for him. He is on record at the beginning of 1996 wondering whether his little team could afford to buy mobile telephones.

In reality, however, the Bildt operation was doomed not by a lack of funds but by a biased concept of the mission. Like Holbrooke, Bildt had to accept the inherent contradiction: the Croat annexation of part of Hercegovina against the promise to the Muslim government that the Americans would defend and uphold the territorial integrity of a unitary Bosnia.

Kelly tells us in *The New Yorker* [9] that, a few days before Dayton, Holbrooke rang him up and said it could be assumed that, sooner or later, the Bosnian Serbs would opt to link up with Serbia. Holbrooke had worked with Henry Kissinger in the final stages of the Vietnam war and recalled that Kissinger predicted that the north would ultimately gobble up the south. What Kissinger needed then — and what Holbrooke felt he needed now — was a "decent interval" to soften up American opinion. The "decent interval" would now seem to be in progress.

It is more than two years since President Clinton gave the green light to the Ayatollahs of Iran, enabling them to penetrate, train and arm the Bosnian Muslims. As William Safire wrote in *The New York Times* [10]: "There was one crucial piece of intelligence that the State Department, the National Security Council and the CIA knew and withheld: that the arms were coming to the Bosnian Muslims from Iran with the President's personal authorisation". The White House has conceded covert operations and in April 1996 ordered an internal investigation into how and why these had happened.

It may already be too late to prevent the Americans from repeating the fatal error which they made in Afghanistan. There, in the period before the Soviet army withdrew (1979), the Americans lavished arms and cash on any Muslim group — provided only that it was anti-Soviet. The groups then turned on each other and dragged Afghanistan down into its present anarchy and chaos.

## Footnotes

1. Kelly, Michael (6 November 1995). *The New Yorker.*

2. *Ibid.*

3. *Ibid.*

4. Alija Izetbegović, TV Bosnia and Hercegovina, Sarajevo, in Serbo-Croat 2045 gmt 6 April 1996.

5. Kelly, Michael (6 November 1995). *The New Yorker.*

6. *Ibid.*

7. Croatian Radio, Zagreb, in Serbo-Croat 1500 gmt, 18 April 1996.

8. Boyd, General Charles G. (September / October 1995). Foreign Affairs, Volume 74, No. 5.

9. Kelly, Michael (6 November 1995). *The New Yorker.*

10. Safire, William (18 April 1996). *The New York Times.*

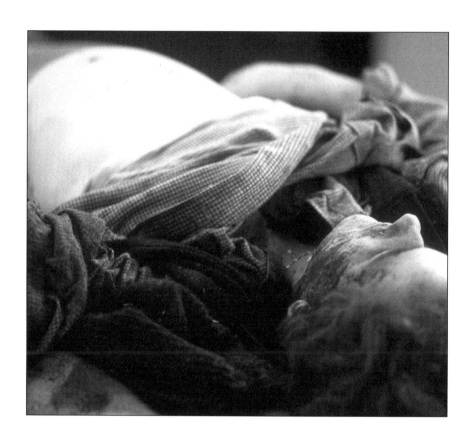

Pregnant woman killed by shelling.
Brčko, Republika Srpska. 11 May 1994.

# Epilogue:

# The Lessons to be Learnt from the Yugoslav Experience

The first lesson is that no foreign country — or international institution — should ever intrude into the affairs of any troubled territory, in any part of the world, without a careful investigation of the causes and origins of the conflict. In the case of Yugoslavia, the EC, UN and Western governments weighed in without any grasp of why the fighting started. The intrusion has been both reckless and counterproductive.

In the specific case of Bosnia and Hercegovina we need to understand, as Major-General Lewis MacKenzie and others have told us[1], that all three of the communities are terrified that their own people may be physically obliterated. Outsiders can only help by mediating a self-enforcing deal. The Bosnian Serb and Bosnian Croat minorities can fall back for protection on their own hinterlands — the states of Serbia and Croatia. Though the Bosnian Muslims cannot have more than their own limited segment of Bosnia and Hercegovina, they have every right to insist that this territory be equally secure. The presence of Turkish troops might provide the kind of protection which the Bosnian Muslims could accept.

Above all, the experience of Yugoslavia should lead us to confront realities. We must abandon "multi-ethnic" and integrationist rhetoric and, instead, admit that the "ethnic cleansing" practised by all three groups is a true reflection of distrust. After four years of fighting, we have to accept that, provisionally at least, most of the peoples living in ex-Yugoslavia prefer to live under the governance and control of members of their own community.

In the longer run, it may be reasonable to hope for a waning of hatreds. In the immediate future, however, we should facilitate the population movements which are still continuing. Too much damage has been done by ignorant and arrogant outsiders who pay no attention to the feelings and fears of the local peoples.

The real obstacle to peace in the winter of 1996 was the appointment of Carl Bildt, the man selected to be the supervisor of the peace. This Swedish diplomat, selected with American approval, claims that there is no alternative to a unitary state of Bosnia and Hercegovina under the Izetbegović presidency. What he failed to understand is that Bosnia and Hercegovina is not — and never has been — a single state nor a single nation.

Whatever the outside world would like, neither the Bosnian Serbs nor the Bosnian Croats will agree to be incorporated into a Bosnian state under the Izetbegović presidency. It is the Christians, Roman Catholic and Orthodox combined, who represent a majority of the population in Bosnia Hercegovina. No solution is feasible unless their interests are seen to be defended.

As we have seen, Alija Izetbegović is no newcomer to the political scene. Tito, seeing the dangers pan-Islam might represent, had Izetbegović jailed for subversive writings. Tito's successors also detected the danger and Izetbegović did not come into his own until Yugoslavia collapsed. In 1981, Izetbegović's ruling party, the SDA, adopted *The Islamic Declaration* [2] as a founding document. When Izetbegović was elected president, his first foreign visits were to the Islamic leaders in the Middle East and Asia.

A lot of nonsense has been written fabricating a "Bosnian tradition" or the "historical continuity" of a Bosnian state. No-one has been more responsible for this distortion than Noel Malcolm, who wrote *Bosnia: A Short History* [3]. Relying primarily on the writings and say-so of Croat *émigrés*, Malcolm would have the reader believe that a Bosnian state has survived since the Middle Ages, and that the Serbs were late arrivals. Malcolm's book was the first to be published during the present conflict, and its thesis has been widely accepted.

On the American side, President Clinton remains unaware of the inherent contradiction in his Bosnian policy. Although the Americans are acutely aware of the threat posed by Muslim fundamentalism, Clinton has publicly committed the Americans to train, equip and arm the Izetbegović army. Even with American support, it has to be recognised that it is unlikely that the Bosnian Muslim army could win the war. The trouble is that the Americans have deprived Izetbegović of any inducement to engage in direct negotiations with the leaders of the Serb and Croat communities. Yet it is difficult to see how, without direct inter-community negotiations, there can be any chance of inter-community reconciliation.

Four years of war have, of course, exacerbated inter-ethnic hostilities. There is now less hope than ever that peace can be negotiated without international mediation. This does not, however, imply a peace imposed from outside ex-Yugoslavia. What the Western leaders have to recognise is that, in the present conflict, all three communities fear for their own survival. All the recent measurements of the will of the peoples, including the latest elections, confirm the centrifugal trends.

Western leaders cannot, of course, remain indifferent to this turbulent corner of Europe. But what they need to seek out are the non-military contributions they can make towards peace. One vital function is to continue the task of monitoring events from the ground.

During the elections of October 1996, the monitors included a former British officer, Michael Shuttleworth. A veteran of many missions to ex-Yugoslavia and Bulgaria, Shuttleworth monitored the elections from Banja Luka. He reported having witnessed vote-rigging on the Bosnian Muslim side: large pre-packed sacks of ballot papers arrived during the count, each paper neatly folded into four, revealing that nobody had ever put these into a ballot box. This trickery could not be exposed because President Clinton vetoed any challenge which might damage the Muslim case.

The West picked on the Bosnian Serbs' political leader, Radovan Karadžić, and military leader, General Ratko Mladić, as the principal enemies. This led them to support Slobodan Milošević, relying on him to help undermine Bosnian Serb support for their own government. In this endeavour, Milošević has so far failed. Most Bosnian Serbs continue to back their own leaders and Shuttleworth tells us that he has witnessed the "increasing professionalism" of the Mladić army.

The Hague Tribunal has failed to find any document indicating that either Karadžić or Mladić ordered troops to commit atrocities. Instead, it has fallen back on allegations that they were responsible for starting the war. The Tribunal has, however, failed to take into account that these leaders were chosen for their ability to resist the incorporation of the Bosnian Serbs into an Izetbegović-led Bosnia and Hercegovina.

In October 1996, under French sponsorship, Milošević recognised Bosnia and Hercegovina as a single state under the Izetbegović presidency. In doing so, he was fully supported by Carl Bildt. The Western media has backed Bildt, and refused to examine any feasible alternative. The British public, relying on fifty-second TV soundbites, has been left confused and unaware of the true reasons why the fighting started.

It cannot be said too often that the war in Bosnia was the direct consequence of the collapse of Yugoslavia. Civil war was inevitable once the Serbs outside Serbia refused to yield, and preferred to fight rather than to be annexed by Tuđman's Croatia or Izetbegović's Bosnia.

Since 1991, three million people in ex-Yugoslavia, out of a population of 24 million, have become refugees. Some fled abroad while others have moved into areas controlled by members of their own ethnic / religious communities. Instead of reconciling themselves to this understandable preference and accommodating it, the Western media has gone on backing a unitary state of Bosnia and Hercegovina. Worse still, it has refused to acknowledge that there is any other way forward.

## Footnotes

1. MacKenzie, Major-General Lewis (1993). *Peacekeeper: The Road to Sarajevo*. Douglas & McIntyre, Vancouver / Toronto.

2. Izetbegović, Alija (republished 1990) *The Islamic Declaration*. Sarajevo.

3. Malcolm, Noel (1994). *Bosnia: A Short History*. Macmillan.

# References

Avakumović, Ivan (1996). The Bully on the Block: American Policy in the Former Yugoslavia. *Second Annual Regional Conference on Russian, East European and Central Asian Studies*, University of Washington, Seattle.

Bell, Martin (1995). *In Harm's Way — Reflections of a War Zone Thug*. Hamish Hamilton, London.

Beloff, Nora (1985). *Tito's Flawed Legacy*. Gollancz.

Beloff, Nora (1979). *Inside the Soviet Empire: Myth and Reality*. New York Times Books.

Beloff, Nora (1963). *The General Says No*. Penguin.

Bogdanović, Dimitrije (1985). *Knjiga o Kosovu* [*The Book of Kosovo*]. Serbian Academy of Sciences and Arts.

Boyd, General Charles G. (September / October 1995). *Foreign Affairs*, Volume 74, No. 5.

Čavoški, Kosta (1996). Evil Curse of Despotic Government, *The South Slav Journal*, Volume 17, No. 1-2 (63-64).

Čavoški, Kosta (April 1995). *Dialogue*.

Čehajić, Rusmir Mahmud (27th April 1994). *Muslim News*.

Djilas, Milovan (22 March 1984). *Osmica*.

Djilas, Milovan (1980). *Tito: The Story from Inside.* Harcourt Brace Jovanovich.

Drew, Elizabeth (1994). *On The Edge: The Clinton Presidency.* Simon and Shuster.

Glenny, Misha (1992). *The Fall of Yugoslavia.* Penguin.

Goebbels, Joseph (1982). *Diaries 1939-1941.* Pan Books, London.

Ignatieff, Michael (29 February 1996). *New York Review of Books.*

Ignatieff, Michael (14 August 1995). *The New Yorker.*

Ivanišević, Milivoje (1994). *Hronika Našeg Groblja — ili slovo o stradanju srpskog naroda Bratunca, Milića, Skelana i Srebrnice* [*The Chronicle of our Graveyards — description of the suffering of the Serbian people of Bratunac, Milići, Skelani and Srebrenica*]. Belgrade.

Izetbegović, Alija (republished 1990). *The Islamic Declaration.* Sarajevo.

Jović, Borislav (1994). *The Last Days of Yugoslavia, Extracts from Diaries.* Belgrade.

Kaplan, Robert D. (1993). *Balkan Ghosts.* St. Martin's Press.

Kelly, Michael (6 November 1995). *The New Yorker.*

Kenney, George (8-15 January 1996). The Nation.

MacKenzie, Major-General Lewis (1993). *Peacekeeper: The Road to Sarajevo.* Douglas & McIntyre, Vancouver / Toronto.

Malcolm, Noel (1994). *Bosnia: A Short History*. Macmillan.

Mamula 1991. *RUSI Journal*, Vol. 136, No. 1.

Mesić, Stipe (1994). *How Yugoslavia was destroyed*. Mislav Press, Zagreb.

Owen, David (1995). *Balkan Odyssey*. Gollancz.

Rushdie, Salman (25 April 1994). *Index on Censorship* 1/2. (reprinted in *The Guardian*).

Schmidt-Eenboom, (1995). *Erich Der Schattenkrieger — Klaus Kinkel und der BND* [acronym for German Military Intelligence]. Econ, Dusseldorf.

Steinberg, Jonathan (1990). *All or Nothing — the Axis and the Holocaust 1941-1943*. Routledge, London / New York.

Tuđman, Franjo (1991). *Croatia at the Crossroads — in Search of a Democratic Confederacy*. Centre for Policy Studies, London.

Vernet, Daniel (1994). *Le Reve Sacrifie*. Editions Odile Jacob, Paris.

West, Rebecca (1942). *Black Lamb and Grey Falcon*. Macmillan.

Wynaendts, Henry (1993). *L'engrenage. Chroniques Yougoslaves Juillet 1991 - Aôut 1992*. Editions Denoel, Paris.

# Index

# About the Author

Nora Beloff joined Reuters in Paris, in 1945, after working for the French Section of the British Political Intelligence Department. In 1947, she became the Paris Correspondent of *The Observer*. She served as the newspaper's correspondent in Moscow and Washington during the 1950s, becoming their Chief Political Correspondent in 1964 (the first woman to hold such a post on a national newspaper). After leaving *The Observer* in 1976 she became an independent roving reporter, writing mainly on the Soviet Union and Eastern Europe.

Her books include: *The General Says No* (1963), an account of Britain's first abortive attempt to join the Common Market; *Transit of Britain* (1973), a discussion of Britain's changing role in the postwar world; *Freedom under Foot* (1976), her protest against the enforcement of trade union membership for journalists proposed by Michael Foot; *No Travel Like Russian Travel* [published in America under the title *Inside the Soviet Empire: Myth and Reality*] (1979), describing her journey by car across the Soviet Union which ended by her being arrested and, finally, of chief importance in connection with the present work, *Tito's Flawed Legacy* (1985).